WILD RICE
for all seasons
COOKBOOK

By Beth Anderson

Illustrations by Jan Anderson

NODIN PRESS

Thirteenth Printing

For assistance with this publication we thank:
Marilyn Nielson, St. Paul
Monroe Killy, Minneapolis
"The Minnesota Archeologist"

Library of Congress Number 82-227709

ISBN 1-932472-26-6

UPC 887077000238

Nodin Press is a division of Micawber's, Inc.
530 North 3rd Street
Suite 120
Minneapolis, MN, 55401

printed in Canada

Table of Contents

History and Lore
of Wild Rice

Sky-blue lakes lie, sparkling like jewels, in the deep green, lush forests of Minnesota, Wisconsin and the neighboring parts of Canada. And after the ice goes out each spring, limp shoots of an aquatic grass appear in many of these lakes. By late summer, these grasses stand tall and produce an edible seed.

As fall and winter approach, game birds stop to eat and rest in the tall grasses of these lakes, by now surrounded by the seasonal gold and red colors that herald the coming of winter.

The American Indians named the edible seed that nature provided in these lakes, wild rice.

And as early as the first century, A.D., they came to the lakes and the connecting streams that criss-cross the glacier-sculptured region to harvest, dry and thresh wild rice, which became the major source of carbohydrate in their diets.

However the wild rice is not a rice at all, but rather the grain-like seed of an aquatic grass, zizania aquatica, which the woodland Indians soon called their "precious wild rice."

By the 1300's and 1400's, these people set up camps along the lake shores late each summer to gather the wild rice, which often was credited with their survival through the long, cold winters. Moving to the camps each year became a highlight, almost a ritual in their culture.

But, wild rice was to become the cause of wars in future years.

During the 1700's, the westward-migrating Chippewas (or Ojibwas) fought many battles with the Fox, Winnebago and Sioux Indians over the control of the wild rice-producing areas.

The Chippewas won and wild rice became the food to which their good health and large stature was attributed.

But the wild rice crop was not always reliable, reportedly producing good crops only three out of four years. And in the years when wild rice was not plentiful, the Chippewas would often go hungry, and sometimes starve during the snowy winters.

Yet, still today, the Chippewas call their wild rice, "precious." However, their automobiles have made the lake-side wild rice camps obsolete. Now they commute from their homes to the lakes to harvest the grain. Many of the older people feel that their culture and heritage would be stronger if the customs of the wild rice camp were revived.

Had you had the opportunity to observe a wild rice camp in the days past, or go to museum displays of a wild rice camp, you would witness a scene much like this:

Temporary birch bark-covered housing, usually open-ended because the weather was still warm, clustered around the drying and threshing operations. Lined up on the lakeshore were birch bark canoes, with the long forked poles that were used to propel the canoes through the shallow waters.

The wild rice was gathered by the Indian women who used a short stick or pole to hold the tall grass over the canoe while another short pole was used to knock the ripened grains off into the bottom of the boat. The men would pole the canoes through the water.

Long ago it was the custom of some Indian tribes to wrap the wild rice, before the grains ripened, with ropes of straw. Sometimes a chain of the tied wild rice was made to establish territories for harvesting once the grain ripened. This custom also reduced the loss of ripe grain to wind, rain or birds.

The harvested rice was laid on woven straw mats to dry several days in the sun and then parched in metal or iron containers set over or near a fire. The partially-filled container was stirred often as the heat from the fire dried the grains.

Another method used was setting the grains on a screen over a fire, much like the Indians dried their fruits and sometimes, their meats.

The threshing usually was done by the young men, who treaded with moccasin-shod feet on the dried rice, which was in a small, skin-lined hole dug into the ground. Two small trees are secured so that he could lean on them as he threshed the rice.

The chaff removed by the threshing was then separated from the wild rice by what the Indians called winnowing. This was sometimes done by pouring the threshed rice from one birch bark basket into another in light breezes, which would blow the chaff from the rice.

Without the breeze, the wild rice was fanned as it was poured from one container to another.

If the breezes were brisk, the threshed rice was simply laid out on a blanket and the wind would blow away the lighter chaff.

Once the winnowing had separated the chaff from the finished wild rice, it was bagged. Sometimes these bags were wrapped in skins and buried deep in the cool earth for winter, or longer, storage.

The wild rice camp scene, just described, involved the adults in all of the stages of wild rice processing and in preparing the meals for the groups. The young children would often be at play or busy gathering wood for the fires.

The Chippewas used the wild rice as a cereal with blueberries, stuffed it into game birds, or cooked the grain in soups or stews with bear, venison, fish or other game. It was as important to them then as wheat and oats are today to the white man, even though the Indians are as likely to rely on super-market foods today as are their countrymen.

The commercialization of wild rice began in the early 1600's when the voyageurs and fur traders began to follow the natural eating patterns of the Indians living in the Upper Great Lakes Region. That primarily was a diet of game and fish with wild rice and wild berries.

By the nineteenth century wild rice was sold to a few

homesteaders. And some enterprising businessmen even advertised and sold the wild rice around the turn of the century for as much as 40 cents a pound.

Numerous and varied methods of wild rice harvesting, processing and marketing have been tried in the last 50 years. But, because the crop grew wild in nature, it was not always reliable. Businessmen went broke as the prices of wild rice fluctuated widely, depending upon the quantity of the harvest.

If water levels were not right, if the stand of the rice was too thick, if the rains and winds came when the grain was ripened, but not yet harvested... All of these factors could mean disaster for the wild rice businessmen, just as the same variables had meant hunger or starvation for his Indian predecessors.

Far-sighted agricultural experts and wild rice businessmen soon realized that the wild rice production would have to be made more consistent before the crop would ever become a viable food for areas outside the midwest United States. The continued dependency on the naturally-produced wild rice would confine it to either the area in which it was produced, the tables of the rich or for restaurant use.

So during the 1950's, wild rice production in low-lying paddies, which were sometimes flooded much like in the production of white rice, was begun.

Equipment was modified to meet the specific needs of growing this temperamental grain. And research was begun to develop strains that would ripen at once and be more resistant to insects and disease.

In the mid 1970's almost three-fourths of the Minnesota wild rice production, which accounted for about 95 percent of the total, was produced in the cultivated wild rice paddies.

National and international marketing efforts, plus the extensive use of wild rice as a gourmet food gift item, are increasing both the awareness and appreciation of the rich, dark, nutritious grain.

And the times have passed when the delicacy, wild rice, is overlooked on buffet tables across the country — simply because no one knew what it was.

Wild rice is now on the lists of accepted items at customs points all over the world, instead of sometimes being held as an "unknown" and "suspect" item in some places.

And just as Americans have learned that turkey is good all year round, for all occasions, the use of wild rice is expanding beyond the traditional stuffings, side dishes and casseroles.

In the 1980's, sales of wild rice are increasing because of the heightened interest in nutrition, health and improved dietary standards.

Nutritional analysis shows that wild rice is low in calories and fat, yet high in fiber and good quality protein. It also has a wide variety of minerals and vitamins. (See the next chapter for more nutrition information.)

These nutritional characteristics, combined with the fact that few wild rice products have any preservatives or additives, make wild rice appealing to a growing number of vegetarians.

On the other hand, wild rice has its own uniqueness as a historical, natural food and as an extraordinary, sophisticated food. It is this special combination that many amateur and professional culinary experts are searching for.

For these same reasons, restaurants are courting their customers with wild rice on the menu more frequently than ever before. Of course, restaurants also like the profitability resulting from the surprisingly low cost-per-serving figures of wild rice. (See details in the next chapter.)

Naturally, wild rice growers, marketers and processors are expanding to meet their widening markets. In Canada, Ontario, Manitoba and Nova Scotia wild rice marketers are becoming more aggressive in the management and harvesting of the wild rice crops from their lakes.

In the United States, some wild rice is being grown in paddies in Northern California, in lakes in Idaho and in wet lowlands on the East Coast. This has spread wild rice production from the Atlantic to the Pacific. Marketing and sales of wild rice is being carried out worldwide.

Surely this would please the wild rice enthusiast, A .E. Jenks, who in 1889 wrote, "If wild rice could be cultivated with any certainty it would be a staple for the white population of America as it has been for the many thousands of Indians before them."

Wild Rice Nutrition and Basic Cooking Directions

American Indians knew that those who ate wild rice were larger and healthier than their neighbors who did not have this nutritious carbohydrate. In Northern Minnesota and Wisconsin and the adjacent parts of Canada, wild rice grows well. And, for the Chippewa Indians who lived there, a winter without a good supply of wild rice to go with their diet of game and dried berries meant that they went hungry . . . or starved.

What the Indians of yesteryears didn't know is that wild rice is a low-calorie, low-fat, high-fiber carbohydrate which supplies appreciable amounts of good quality protein, plus minerals and vitamins.

Then, and today, wild rice meets the nutritional requirements people are looking for.

Calorie counters know that a half-cup of wild rice has only about 70 calories. And vegetarians count on the protein in wild rice.

As with other cereal and grain products, wild rice protein is not a complete protein (one that has all the essential amino acids). Wild rice should be combined or served with complete protein—even small amounts of cheese, eggs, meats or nuts will do—to supply complete protein to the body.

Composition of Wild Rice and Other Selected Cereal Products

Components (Percent)	Wild Rice	Brown Rice	Polished White Rice	Oats	Hard Red Winter Wheat	Corn
Water	8.5	12.0	12.0	8.3	12.5	13.8
Protein	14.1	7.5	6.7	14.2	12.3	8.9
Fat	.7	1.9	.4	7.4	1.8	3.9
Ash	1.4	1.2	.5	1.9	1.7	1.2
Crude Fiber	1.0	.9	.3	1.2	2.3	2.0
Total Carbohydrate	75.3	77.4	80.4	68.2	71.7	72.2
Minerals (mg/100g)						
Calcium	19	32	24	53	46	22
Phosphorus	339	221	94	405	354	268
Iron	4.2	1.6	.8	4.5	3.4	2.1
Potassium	220.	214	92	352	370	284
Vitamins						
Vitamin A (I.U.)	0	0	0	0	0	0
Thiamine (mg/100g)	.45	.34	.07	.60	.52	.37
Riboflavin (mg/100g)	.63	.05	.03	.14	.12	.12
Niacin (mg/100g)	6.2	4.7	1.6	1.0	4.3	2.2
Vitamin C (mg./100g)	0	0	0	0	0	0

Chart courtesy of the Minnesota Wild Rice Council; data from USDA Handbook No. 8

Because wild rice increases in volume as much as four times when cooked, comparing the cost-per-serving, rather than the cost-per-pound, is a good way to figure its actual price. Here are some equivalents for wild rice: one pound wild rice measures about two and three-fourths cups. One cup wild rice increases to about four cups when cooked, enough for six servings. One pound wild rice will expand to about 10 to 12 cups cooked rice, or enough for 20 to 24 servings.

There are no nation-wide grading systems for wild rice now, although most processors and marketers designate the rice according to size. These commercial designations usually are, in descending order: select, extra fancy, fancy, thin grain and sometimes, broken. The last two, thin grain and broken, are seldom on retail supermarket shelves, except in some processed foods.

The larger or darker the kernel of wild rice is, or if the rice is old, the longer it will take to cook. Because of this, it is best to follow cooking instructions that come with the rice. However, the basic directions and recipes here can be used with any wild rice, so long as the cooking time is adjusted as needed.

The rice should be cooked until it puffs and the inner, lighter part is visible. Over-cooking increases volume, but makes the rice mushy. Sometimes undercooking, to achieve a chewy, more nut-like texture, is desirable, like for some cold salads. If the cooked wild rice is to be used in a casserole or food combination to be cooked later, it should be cooked only until the grains puff open and not until the wild rice softens totally.

If you're experiencing the deliciously different flavor of wild rice for the first time, you can remove small spoonfuls of wild rice at several stages during the final cooking. This helps you judge the stages of doneness and how you like it.

Soaking the wild rice in water overnight, or pouring boiling water over it and letting it stand for 30 minutes, will decrease cooking time and increase the volume of the cooked rice.

Uncooked wild rice can be stored in a tightly covered container set in cool place for several months; however for longer storage, it is best refrigerated in a tightly closed container.

Cooked wild rice, well-drained and without other foods added, will keep in a tightly covered container, refrigerated for several weeks or it can be frozen for longer storage.

To simplify cooking, prepare wild rice one pound at a time in advance. Then use some of it and refrigerate another portion for use within a few days. Freeze the remainder for use in the near future. Many of the recipes in the following sections of this book call for cooked wild rice. If you keep cooked wild rice on hand, it's both quick and simple to serve up these interesting foods.

Here are basic directions for cooking wild rice, and several standard recipes for wild rice side dishes. For other recipes, see the seasonal sections that follow.

BASIC WILD RICE

1 cup Wild Rice
4 cups water
1 tsp. salt

Wash rice thoroughly. Place the wild rice, water and salt in a 3-qt. heavy saucepan and bring to a boil. Reduce heat, cover and simmer 45 to 60 minutes, or until rice has puffed and most of liquid has been absorbed. Fluff rice with a fork and cook, uncovered, to evaporate any excess liquid. Makes about 4 cups rice.

VARIATIONS: Substitute beef or chicken bouillon for the water, omitting salt. Substitute 1 cup white wine for 1 cup water.

STEEPED WILD RICE

Pour 4 cups boiling water over 1 cup washed wild rice and let stand for 30 minutes. Drain and add another 4 cups boiling water and let stand 30 minutes. Repeat this process two more times, adding 4 tsp. salt to the last water. Drain. Keep wild rice hot in top of double broiler. Stir in 1 to 2 tsp. butter and additional salt, to taste, before serving. Makes 4 cups.

PRE-SOAKED WILD RICE

Cover wild rice with water and let stand at room temperature overnight. Drain and wash with fresh water. Proceed with any method of basic preparation. Cooking time will be shortened slightly and the volume of the rice will be slightly more. (For quicker method: pour boiling water over wild rice and let set 30 minutes. Drain and proceed with basic preparation.)

WILD RICE FOR COLD SALADS

Toss 4 cups cooked wild rice with about 1 tbsp. cooking oil. This helps keep the grains of rice from sticking together.

WILD RICE
to go with game or poultry

1 medium onion, chopped
2 tbsp. butter
1 cup Wild Rice
4 cups chicken broth
1/4 tsp. each sage, thyme and marjoram
Salt, if needed

Saute the onion in the butter in a heavy 3-qt. saucepan. Add the wild rice, spices, and broth. Bring to a boil. Cover, reduce heat and simmer 45 to 60 minutes, or until most of the liquid has been absorbed. Fluff rice with a fork. Salt, if needed. Cook, uncovered, to evaporate any excess moisture. Makes about 4 cups rice.

WILD RICE
with mushrooms and bacon

6 slices bacon, cut-up
1/2 lb. sliced fresh mushrooms
1 cup Wild Rice
4 cups chicken broth
Salt, if needed

Fry the bacon in a heavy 3-qt. saucepan. Remove bacon, drain and crumble. Saute the mushrooms and wild rice in the bacon drippings about 3 minutes. Add the chicken broth. Bring to a boil. Cover and reduce heat to a simmer. Simmer 45 to 60 minutes, or until rice is puffed and tender. Fluff rice with a fork. Salt, if needed. Cook, uncovered, to evaporate any excess moisture. Add crumbled bacon, tossing lightly to mix. Makes about 6 cups.

Wild rice cooks well in any microwave oven that has both a high- and low-power setting. But, because wild rice requires the longer simmering time, the microwave oven does not reduce the cooking time drastically.

It is best to follow the manufacturers' directions for cooking wild rice. Lacking these, use the following basic directions, making adjustments in time, according to the power of your microwave oven.

MICROWAVED WILD RICE

Place 1 cup wild rice in a 3-qt. glass covered casserole. Add 4 cups water and 1 tsp. salt. Microwave on high about 6 minutes, then reduce power setting to low, or defrost, and microwave 30 minutes. Leave rice undisturbed in oven for another 10 to 15 minutes. Check to be sure that rice is tender.

(Any of the basic directions and standard recipes above can be adapted to the microwave oven. And many of the recipes that follow in this book also work well in the microwave oven, but you should make time adjustments suitable for your particular oven, using the manufacturers' directions and recipes as a guideline.)

● ●

Because many nutrition and health studies show that excessive salt and sugar are not healthful, most of the recipes that follow in this book call for these ingredients in adequate, but not excessive amounts. Tasting and adjusting final seasoning is one of the secrets of a good cook. But remember that, if you oversalt, it's not healthful and the recipe did not specify it.

Wild Rice Recipes for Spring

Minneapolis, Minn. hostess Joan Soskin combines Chinese pea pods with jicama (Mexican potato) slices in a wild rice side dish that is a favorite with both family and guests.

If your supermarket doesn't have jicama or fresh Chinese pea pods, substitute sliced water chestnuts and frozen Chinese pea pods.

SOSKIN WILD RICE SAUTE

1/2 cup (1 stick) butter
2 garlic cloves, pressed
1 cup small slices jicama (water chestnuts can be substituted)
1/4 lb. fresh Chinese pea pods, (or a 6-oz. pkg. frozen Chinese pea pods, slightly thawed)
1/4 tsp. white pepper, or to taste
1/4 tsp. salt, or to taste
4 to 6 cups cooked Wild Rice, 1 to 1 1/2 cups uncooked

In a heavy skillet, melt butter over medium heat and saute the garlic with the jicama and the pea pods 3 to 4 minutes, turning gently with a spatula from time to time. Be careful not to break jicama or pea pods. When pea pods are still quite crisp, sprinkle with white pepper and salt and stir in wild rice. Continue cooking, covered, just until the pea pods are tender-crisp and the wild rice, heated through. Serves 6 to 10, depending upon the amount of wild rice used.

When first you find the earliest baby green peas of Spring, cook them until just done and then toss with this wild rice casserole with toasted slivered almonds. It's an excellent accompaniment to fish or lamb.

WILD RICE PETIT POIS

2 cups tiny green peas, cooked until just tender, (about 1½ to 2 lbs. fresh peas)
4 cups cooked Wild Rice, about 1 cup uncooked
3 tbsp. butter
1/2 cup finely sliced almonds
1 tbsp. grated orange rind

Prepare the peas and the wild rice. Melt the butter in a 2-qt. casserole and lightly toss the almonds in this. Bake almonds in a 325 degree oven, 10 to 15 minutes, stirring frequently, until almonds are lightly toasted. Add the peas, drained, and wild rice with orange rind to casserole and toss lightly to mix. Bake, uncovered, at 325 degrees until all ingredients are heated through. Serves 6.

Wild Rice Almondine is delicious year 'round, but it is particularly good with lamb, veal or fresh fish in the early spring.

WILD RICE ALMONDINE

1 cup Wild Rice, cooked with 2 cups chicken broth and
  2 cups white wine, according to basic or package
  directions
1/2 cup (1 stick) butter, not margarine
1 cup blanched slivered almonds, toasted until a light
  golden brown
Salt, to taste

Saute the cooked wild rice in the butter melted in a large skillet. Stir in the toasted almonds and adjust seasoning, if needed. Serves 6.

VARIATIONS: Stir in fresh avocado cubes, sauteed pea pods, water chestnuts, chopped jicama or artichoke bottoms, or a combination of these.

This wild rice hot dish, with chicken or turkey, requires very little advance preparation.

WILD RICE HOT DISH WITH CHICKEN

1 cup Wild Rice
2 cups cooked, cut-up chicken or turkey
1 (10½-oz.) can chicken broth

2 tbsp. chop suey or soy sauce
1 (10½-oz.) can mushroom soup
2 cups water
2 ribs celery, sliced
2 large onions, chopped
1/4 green pepper, chopped
1/2 cup chopped olives (green or ripe)
1 cup frozen peas
1/2 cup blanched slivered almonds

Combine all ingredients in a 3-qt. buttered casserole. Mix well. Cover and bake 2 hours at 325 degrees. Uncover, fluff with a fork and bake, uncovered, until rice is tender and moisture absorbed. Serves 8 to 10.

The saute of wild rice and spinach with other vegetables can be a colorful addition to the first cookout of the season.

WILD RICE SPINACH SAUTE

1/2 cup (1 stick) butter
1/4 cup chopped fresh chives
1/4 cup chopped fresh parsley
2 cups chopped fresh spinach
1/2 cup mild red-skinned radishes, thinly sliced
4 cups cooked Wild Rice, about 1 cup uncooked
1 to 1 1/2 tsp. salt, to taste
1 tbsp. sherry, optional

In a large skillet, melt the butter and saute the chives, parsley and spinach just until they begin to become limp. Stir in the radish slices and wild rice. Reduce heat and continue to cook just until warm. Stir in salt and sherry, if used. Serve hot. Serves 6.

Betty Koke, Portsmouth, Virginia, shared a recipe that inspired this adaptation for Beefy Wild Rice with Mushrooms. It's well seasoned with double-strength beef bouillon so it goes best with beef or pork, rather than lighter entrees of chicken, veal, lamb or fish.

BEEFY WILD RICE WITH MUSHROOMS

1 cup Wild Rice
2 cups double-strength beef bouillon
1/4 to 1/2 tsp. freshly ground black pepper
1 tbsp. butter
1/2 lb. fresh mushrooms, sliced

Soak the wild rice in cold water for an hour before cooking. Drain the rice and place in a 2½-qt. casserole. Pour the bouillon over and add the pepper. Cover and bake in a 350-degree oven for 30 minutes. Melt the butter in a skillet and saute the mushrooms just until they begin to soften. Stir the mushrooms into the rice. Cover and continue to cook in a 350-degree oven another 30 minutes, or until rice is popped and tender. Stir rice with a fork and serve to 4 or 6.

When you want to add real class to meatballs, add
wild rice. They'll be just as good as meatballs are
supposed to be, but extra fancy because of the wild
rice and the wine sauce.

WILD RICE MEATBALLS

1 lb. ground beef
1 small onion, finely chopped
1/2 cup Wild Rice
1/2 tsp. seasoned salt
1/2 tsp. garlic salt
1/3 cup fine dry bread crumbs
3/4 cup evaporated milk
Oil, for frying
1 (10¾-oz.) can cream of mushroom soup
1/2 soup can water
1/2 soup can dry white wine
1/2 tsp. salt
1/8 tsp. freshly ground black pepper, or to taste
1/4 tsp. sage

Combine the ground beef with the onion, rice,
seasoned and garlic salts, bread crumbs and milk,
mixing briefly and lightly, but thoroughly. Shape
into about 4 doz. meatballs, 1-inch in diameter.
Brown lightly on all sides in a small amount of oil
in skillet set over medium-high heat. Mix mushroom
soup with the water and wine, salt, pepper and sage.
Pour this over meatballs. Cover and simmer over very
low heat about 1½ hours, or bake, covered, in a 275
degree oven about 1¼ hours. Serves 4.

This puffy main dish of vegetables, wild rice and eggs makes an entree that's delightfully different—it's adapted from a Mid-Eastern recipe. But, it's pleased a few meat-and-potatoes people, so try it soon.

MID-EASTERN WILD RICE BAKE

2 cups cooked Wild Rice, about 1/2 cup uncooked
2 cups finely chopped leek
1 cup finely chopped parsley
1 cup finely chopped green onion
1 cup finely chopped fresh spinach, or 1 (9- or 10-oz.)
    pkg. frozen chopped spinach, thawed and drained
    well
1 1/2 tsp. salt
1/2 tsp. pepper
1 1/2 tbsp. flour
1/3 cup chopped walnuts
8 eggs, lightly beaten
1/3 cup butter
Plain yogurt

Combine the wild rice, leek, parsley, green onion and spinach with the salt, pepper, flour and walnuts. Add the eggs and mix well. Melt the butter in an 8-inch square pan. Pour the mixture into the pan and bake at 325 degrees for an hour, or until the top is crisp and lightly browned. Serve as a main dish with yogurt. Serves 8.

This puff-topped wild rice dish can be either entree for luncheons or suppers or a filling side dish to accompany a heartier dinner entree. Frozen chopped spinach—thawed, cooked and drained—could be substituted for the parsley.

WILD RICE PUFF

3 tbsp. butter
2 ribs celery, sliced
3 cups cooked Wild Rice, about 2/3 cup uncooked
1/2 cup freshly grated Parmesan cheese
1/2 cup finely chopped fresh parsley
3 hard-cooked eggs, chopped
1/2 tsp. each salt and celery salt
2 egg whites, beaten until soft peaks form
1/2 cup mayonnaise, not salad dressing

Melt the butter in a skillet and saute the celery until softened slightly, 4 to 5 minutes. Combine this with the wild rice, cheese, parsley, chopped eggs, salt and celery salt. Toss to mix well and turn into a lightly greased 1½-qt. casserole.

(Casserole can be prepared ahead to this point, covered and refrigerated. However, reheat casserole before spreading egg white-mayonnaise mixture on top.)

When ready to finish and serve, fold the mayonnaise into the stiffly beaten egg whites and spread this over the hot rice mixture in casserole. Broil until topping is lightly browned and puffed. Serves 6.

Tender asparagus spears are added to this casserole during the final baking to make it a meal almost complete in itself. Add a fruit or tossed salad, bread, beverage and a simple dessert for a satisfying, yet simple meal.

When asparagus is not in season, outline the casserole with broccoli flowerettes for the same colorful, complete casserole.

SPRING-TIME WILD RICE CASSEROLE WITH ASPARAGUS AND CHICKEN

1 cup Wild Rice
2 cups chicken broth
1 (2- to 3-oz.) jar mushroom slices and juice
2 tbsp. butter
6 chicken breast halves
1/2 envelope onion recipe and soup mix
1 (10½-oz.) can cream of mushroom soup, diluted
   with 1/4 cup water
1 1/2 lb. fresh aspargus spears, or 30 spears
1/4 cup (1/2 stick) butter, melted
Paprika

Soak the wild rice overnight in cold water, or pour boiling water over rice and let stand 30 minutes. Drain rice and spread in a 9x11-inch shallow baking container. Pour chicken broth over; add mushrooms and juices and dot with the butter. Place chicken breasts in the center of casserole. Sprinkle onion soup mix over all. Spread the slightly diluted mushroom soup over the chicken breasts. Bake, uncovered, at 350 degrees an hour.

Meanwhile trim asparagus stalks up until they cut easily. When casserole has baked for an hour, arrange asparagus spears around edges of casserole. Brush the asparagus lightly with melted butter. Sprinkle all the casserole lightly with paprika. Cover and bake 30 to 45 minutes longer, or until asparagus and chicken are tender. Serves 6.

All the fixin' for this dinner is done at least an hour in advance. And it's nice with fresh pineapple, available in most areas during the spring. The pineapple, too, can be cubed in advance, covered tightly and refrigerated.

LOW-CALORIE CHICKEN WITH WILD RICE

2/3 cup Wild Rice, uncooked
1 large green pepper, coarsely chopped
4 ribs celery, coarsely chopped
1 1/2 cups chicken broth or bouillon
4 chicken breast halves
Soy sauce
2 green onions and some of the green tops, finely sliced

Combine the rice with the pepper, celery and chicken broth in a lightly buttered 2 to 2½-qt. casserole. Brush chicken breasts with soy, immerse in rice. Cover and bake at 350 degrees for 1 to 1½ hours or until rice is done.
Serve sprinkled with sliced green onions and pass soy sauce to go over rice and chicken. Serves 4, 1 breast per person.

*This quickie Wild Rice Chicken Bake could be the
one that you rely on when you invite dinner guests
at the last minute.*

*If you have cooked wild rice on hand, you can use
convenience or prepared foods to meet the dinner-
bell deadline. Stop at the supermarket deli or your
favorite fried chicken pick-up establishment for the
chicken, and use a gravy mix to have this casserole
in the oven ... presto!!!*

*Then you have just enough time to toss a salad, set
the table and freshen up yourself before the guests
ring the doorbell.*

QUICKIE WILD RICE CHICKEN BAKE

6 fried chicken breasts or thighs
4 cups cooked Wild Rice, about 1 cup uncooked
2 cups chicken gravy, thinned with 1/2 cup milk
Paprika
Chopped fresh parsley

Arrange the chicken on top of the rice in a shallow
lightly greased casserole. Spoon the gravy over the
chicken and rice; sprinkle with the paprika and some
chopped fresh parsley. Bake, covered, at 350 degrees
about 20 minutes, then uncover and continue baking
5 to 10 minutes. Serves 4 to 6.

With cinnamon, peanuts and raisins, this wild rice and chicken entree has an Oriental flair. Serve it with pea pods sauteed briefly in butter with a touch of garlic. Mandarin orange segments, chilled with a splash of kirsch, make a nice dessert for this meal.

ORIENTAL CHICKEN AND WILD RICE DISH

1 (3- to 4-lb.) chicken
6 cups cooked Wild Rice, about 1 1/2 cups
   uncooked
2 medium onions, sliced
3 tbsp. butter
1/2 cup peanuts
1/2 cup raisins
1 tsp. cinnamon
1 tsp. black pepper

Bake or roast the chicken, seasoning with salt and pepper. Remove meat from carcass in fairly large pieces. Combine this with the rice. Saute the onions in the butter until onions are transparent; then stir in the peanuts and raisins and saute several minutes longer. Sprinkle with the cinnamon and pepper, stirring to distribute these well. Combine the rice and chicken with the sauteed mixture in a lightly buttered 3-qt. casserole. Bake, covered, at 200 degrees 1 hour. (The long cooking enhances the flavor combinations.) Serves 8 to 10.

It's a perfect do-ahead entree for almost any entertaining. But Wild Rice Ham Rolls with Creamy Wine
Sauce is especially nice for buffets because the ham
rolls are easy to cut with a fork.

A fresh green vegetable, a fruit salad and rolls can
complete this simple, yet special meal.

For a variation, tuck pre-cooked, thin asparagus spears
into the ham rolls, along with the creamy rice filling.

WILD RICE HAM ROLLS WITH
CREAMY WINE SAUCE

6 cups cooked Wild Rice, about 1 1/2 cups
   uncooked
1/4 cup snipped fresh parsley
1/4 cup finely sliced green onion or scallion
8 ham slices, about 1/3 inch-thick
For Creamy Wine sauce:
1/4 lb. fresh mushrooms, finely chopped
1/4 cup finely sliced green onion or scallion
1/4 cup (1/2 stick) butter
1/4 cup flour
1/2 tsp. salt
1/4 tsp. each white pepper and nutmeg
1/2 cup dry white wine
1 pint whipping cream

Combine the cooked wild rice with the parsley and onion. Set aside. To make cream sauce, saute the mushrooms and onion in the butter about 3 minutes. Stir in the flour, salt, white pepper and nutmeg, cooking and stirring until blended well. Remove from heat and slowly blend in the wine. Then stir in the cream. Return to heat and, stirring constantly, cook until sauce thickens slightly.

Combine 1 cup of the sauce with 2 cups of the cooked rice. Divide this lengthwise down the center of the ham slices. Place the remaining rice in the bottom of a lightly buttered shallow casserole, about 7x11-inches. Fold the edges of the ham slices over the creamy rice filling and place, seam side down, over the rice. Spoon the remaining sauce over the ham rolls and rice.

This can be covered tightly and refrigerated for baking later.

To reheat, bake uncovered at 350 degrees about 20 minutes, or until food is heated thoroughly and sauce has begun to bubble in the center. Serves 8.

This tuna and wild rice mold is just right for spring-time. And it goes well with fresh asparagus spears and strawberry shortcake.

WILD RICE MOLD WITH TUNA

4 cups cooked Wild Rice, about 1 cup uncooked
2 (6- to 7-oz.) cans tuna
2 tbsp. butter
1 cup sliced fresh mushrooms, about 1/8 lb.
1/4 cup flour
1 1/2 cups milk
1/4 tsp. nutmeg
1/2 tsp. salt
1/4 tsp. dry mustard

Lightly pack the rice, layered with 1 can drained and flaked tuna, in a buttered 1-qt. ring mold. Set mold in a pan and pour hot water, 1-inch deep, into the pan around the mold. Bake at 325 degrees 20 minutes.

Meanwhile, drain oil from remaining can of tuna into a small skillet and add butter to this. Set tuna aside. Saute the mushrooms in the butter and tuna oil about 3 minutes. Sprinkle flour over mushrooms, stirring to blend in flour. Stir in milk, cooking and stirring constantly until mixture thickens slightly. Add nutmeg, salt and mustard and stir in reserved tuna.

Turn rice mold out onto heated serving platter and serve with tuna-mushroom sauce in center. Serves 4.

Except for the cooked wild rice, celery and green pepper all the ingredients for this nice lunch or dinner entree can be kept on hand.

WILD RICE SEAFOOD CASSEROLE

1 cup Wild Rice, cooked in chicken broth, according to
   basic or package directions
1 (10½ oz.) can mushroom soup
4 ribs celery, sliced
1 green pepper, chopped
1 (about 6-oz.) can shrimp, rinsed and drained
1 (about 6-oz.) can crab, rinsed, drained and flaked
1 small jar chopped pimiento, drained
1 (2- to 3-oz.) jar mushroom stems and pieces,
   drained

For sauce:
1 (about 6-oz.) can shrimp, rinsed and drained
1 (10½-oz.) can mushroom soup
1 (2- to 3-oz.) jar mushroom stems and pieces
1 tbsp. sherry

Combine the cooked wild rice with the mushroom soup, which has been stirred until smooth and creamy. Stir in the celery, green pepper, shrimp, crab, pimiento and mushroom stems and pieces. Mix well. Pour into a lightly greased 2-qt. casserole and bake, covered, about 45 minutes at 350 degrees.

Meanwhile, heat the second can of shrimp, mushroom soup and mushroom stems and pieces together with the sherry to make a sauce. Pass this in gravy boat to be served on top of servings of the casserole. Serves 6 to 8.

With a sauce made from cream of mushroom soup, this lobster-topped wild rice is plenty speedy to put together....and special enough to be lunch or dinner for guests. For really simple meals, add French bread and a tossed salad. For dessert, serve scoops of lemon and lime sherbert, topped with a touch of cream de menthe.

CREAMY LOBSTER 'N WILD RICE

3 cups hot cooked Wild Rice, about 2/3 cup
   uncooked
3 tbsp. melted butter
3 tbsp. minced fresh parsley
2 tbsp. finely chopped onion
1 tsp. salt
1 (10¾-oz.) can cream of shrimp soup
1 tbsp. sherry
1 1/2 cups (about 9 oz.) lobster or Alaskan king crab
   meat, flaked
Pinch cayenne pepper, if desired

Combine the rice with the butter, parsley, onion and salt, toss lightly. Cook, covered, until heated through. Stir the soup until creamy and stir in the sherry and crab. Heat gently, adding the cayenne carefully. When hot, serve the lobster sauce on wild rice to 4.

Some of the moss-hung coastal areas of Georgia and South Carolina are low, marshy areas with salt-water rivers, prolific in shrimp and crab. And this "low country" has it's own style of cooking, relying heavily on rice and seafood.

While the traditional "low-country" recipes use white rice, many of them, made with wild rice, make intriguing side dishes to add interest to many different types of dinners.

LOW COUNTRY SHRIMP AND RICE

1/4 cup (1/2 stick) butter
2 cups cooked Wild Rice, about 1/2 cup uncooked
1 lb. cooked shrimp, cut into 1/2-inch pieces

1/2 cup minced water chestnuts
2 eggs, lightly beaten
1 to 2 tbsp. soy sauce, as desired
1 or 2 green onions, chopped with some of the green
    tops

Melt the butter in a large skillet. Add the rice, shrimp and water chestnuts. Cook, stirring frequently, until heated through. Combine the eggs with the soy sauce and add to the heated shrimp and rice mixture, stirring rapidly until eggs are set. Serve with the chopped green onion on top. Serves 6.

A crab stuffing in large mushroom caps, topped with Parmesan cheese and served on wild rice with a Bechamel sauce.....This exquisite entree is the creation of James Blake, who is the owner-chef at Finlayson's Fine Foods, 50th and Penn Ave. S. in Minneapolis, Minn.

But, it's not an everday specialty; "I make this when I can get the extra large mushrooms that are so perfect for the crab stuffing," said Blake.

Some customers ask to be called when this is on Blake's menu.

CRAB-STUFFED MUSHROOMS ON WILD RICE

For crab-stuffed mushrooms:
1 cup (2 sticks) butter
1/4 cup oil
1 large onion, chopped
6 cloves garlic, finely chopped
1/2 cup chopped mushroom stems
1 tsp. basil
1 tsp. salt
1/4 tsp. white pepper
2 tbsp. Dijon-style mustard
Splash white wine
1/2 cup crushed garlic-flavored croutons
1/2 to 3/4 lb. Alaskan king crab meat
2 lbs. large mushrooms for stuffing, with stems removed and chopped

For Bechamel sauce:
2 tbsp. butter
2 tbsp. flour
1/2 tsp. salt
1 cup light cream
4 to 6 cups cooked Wild Rice, 1 to 1 1/2 cups uncooked

Melt the butter with the oil in a skillet and saute the onion, garlic and mushroom pieces, adding basil, salt, pepper, mustard, wine and crouton crumbs. Break up the crab meat and add to the stuffing. Divide the stuffing in the up-turned cavity of the mushroom caps. Place these in a shallow baking dish and sprinkle liberally with the Parmesan cheese. Set aside.

To make Bechamel sauce, melt the butter and stir in the flour with the salt, stirring and cooking over low heat until mixture is blended. Slowly stir in the cream, stirring and cooking until mixture thickens. Stir cooked hot wild rice into this. Adjust seasonings as desired. Keep warm.

Bake the stuffed mushrooms in a very hot oven or at 450 degrees 13 to 15 minutes. For each serving, spoon some of the hot sauced rice onto each serving plate and "nest" 1 or 2 stuffed mushrooms in the rice. Serves 4 to 6.

"This dish of richly sauced crab and wild rice is a good luncheon dish, but I find that men enjoy it as a supper dish also," writes Jeri Jossy, Portland, Oregon, who shared the recipe.

DUNGENESS CRAB AND WILD RICE

1 cup sliced mushrooms
1/2 cup chopped onion
1/4 cup (1/2 stick) butter
1 tsp. salt
1/4 tsp. pepper
1 1/2 lb. crab meat (can reduce amount of crab to
    1/2 lb.)
1 tbsp. English (hot) mustard
1/4 cup sherry
4 cups cooked Wild Rice, about 1 cup uncooked

For sauce:
1/4 cup (1/2 stick) butter
1/4 cup flour
1/2 tsp. salt
1/4 tsp. white pepper
2 cups heavy cream
2 cups milk
1 egg yolk
Parmesan cheese, about 1/4 cup

Saute the mushrooms and onion in the butter 2 to 3 minutes. Add salt, pepper, crab, mustard and sherry, stirring gently so that crab stays in chunks. Set aside.

To make white sauce, melt the second ¼ cup butter in a heavy saucepan and sprinkle in the flour, salt and white pepper. Cook and stir until blended well. Slowly stir in the cream and milk, cooking and stirring constantly until sauce thickens. Stir about half of this into the sauteed onion, mushroom and crab mixture. Divide the rice between six lightly buttered ramekins, or layer in an 8x12-inch shallow baking casserole. Spoon the crab sauce over the rice.

Beat the egg yolk lightly and add to the remaining white sauce; heat gently several minutes, stirring constantly until thickened. Spoon this over the crab sauce and sprinkle with the Parmesan cheese. Bake at 325 degrees about 20 minutes, or until heated through. Serves 6 to 8.

Quick as a wink, that's how fast you can put this wild rice casserole in the oven....where it can cook right along with a beef, pork or lamb roast.

SPEEDY WILD RICE CASSEROLE

1 cup Wild Rice
1 (10½-oz.) can cream of chicken soup
1 (10½-oz.) can cream of mushroom soup
2 soup cans water

Place the wild rice in a buttered 2-qt. casserole. Blend the soups gradually with the water and stir this into wild rice. Cover and bake at 325 to 350 degrees for 3 hours, stirring twice during last hour of cooking and when removed from oven. Let set about 5 minutes before serving. Serves 8.
(Can substitute cream of celery soup.)

When you're lucky enough to have a nice-sized, freshly-caught lake trout, here's a recipe with a wild rice stuffing that's just right for the oven. However, if you want to try it on the grill, here are directions for this, too.

LAKE TROUT WITH WILD RICE STUFFING

1 (2 to 3-lb.) lake trout
Crushed sweet basil leaves
Black pepper

For stuffing:
1/4 lb. pork sausage
1/2 green pepper, chopped
1 rib celery, finely chopped
1 medium onion, finely chopped
1/2 cup fresh sliced mushrooms
2 garlic cloves, finely minced
4 cups cooked Wild Rice, about 1 cup uncooked
1 tsp. celery salt, optional
1/4 tsp. white pepper, optional

Wash and clean the fish thoroughly, leaving it whole with the head on, if desired. Working from the body cavity, debone the fish. Rub the cavity with basil and pepper. Wrap fish in foil or plastic wrap and refrigerate several hours.

To make stuffing, fry the pork sausage, adding the green pepper, celery, onion, mushrooms and garlic to saute during the final stages of frying.

Drain excess fat and stir in the wild rice. Season with the celery salt and pepper, as needed.

Stuff the fish with the stuffing and bake, uncovered, in a very hot oven, 400 to 450 degrees, just until fish is done—when the flesh flakes easily on the side of the fish—about 15 minutes for a 2-lb. fish and about 20 minutes for a 3-lb. fish. Do not overcook.

Using wide spatulas, gently move fish to a warm platter and serve, whole, garnished with lemon wedges, broccoli and boiled new potatoes. A 2-lb. fish will serve 4 to 6 and a 3-lb. one, 6 to 8.

To do this fish on the grill, place stuffed fish on container fashioned from several thicknesses of heavy-duty aluminum foil set on rack about 6 inches over a bed of charcoal. The coals should be burned to the grey ash stage. If grill is covered, close cover and cook about 30 minutes for a 2-lb. fish, and up to 40 minutes, for a 3-lb. fish. Check fish carefully during the final stages of cooking to be sure that it does not overcook. When flesh flakes easily near thickest part of fish, it is done.

Lacking a cover for the grill, fashion a tent of aluminum foil to cover fish and area the size of the pile of charcoals so that the tent will hold some of the heat.

*An English adaptation of an old India dish, kedgeree,
combines salmon with hard-cooked eggs and, in this
version, wild rice. It's nice for almost any meal but is
especially well suited for a late-morning brunch.*

WILD RICE KEDGEREE

2 lbs. fresh salmon
1/4 cup each white wine and water
6 peppercorns
Few sprigs parsley
4 cups cooked Wild Rice, about 1 cup uncooked
1/2 cup (1 stick) butter
1 tbsp. curry powder
6 hard-cooked eggs, coarsely chopped
3/4 cup heavy cream
1 tsp. salt
1/4 tsp. white pepper
1/2 cup chopped fresh parsley

Put the salmon in a casserole and pour the wine and
water over. Scatter the peppercorns and parsley in
the liquid and bake, covered, at 350 degrees for 25
to 30 minutes, or just until the fish flakes easily.
Let cool in the cooking liquid.

Cook the rice according to the basic directions.
Spread in a 11x7-inch lightly greased casserole.

Drain the salmon and flake fish, discarding skin and
any bones.

In a heavy saucepan, melt the butter and stir in the curry and cook gently about 2 minutes, stirring constantly. Add the flaked fish and the chopped eggs. (You can prepare this a day ahead if you refrigerate the rice and fish mixture separately, and tightly covered, at this point.)

To complete recipe, heat the rice and the fish mixture separately and toss the two together, cooking over high heat. Add the cream, salt, pepper and parsley. Adjust seasoning, if necessary. Heat thoroughly and serve at once. Serves 6.

When fish is on the menu, Lemony-Tarragon Wild Rice will be a light, refreshing addition to the menu.

LEMONY-TARRAGON WILD RICE

3 tbsp. butter
1 tbsp. instant chicken bouillon granules
1 tbsp. fresh lemon juice
1 tsp. chopped fresh tarragon
4 cups hot cooked Wild Rice, about 1 cup uncooked
Salt and pepper, to taste

Melt the butter and stir in the bouillon granules, lemon juice and tarragon. Cook over low heat until bouillon granules are dissolved, adding a tablespoon of water, only if necessary. Toss this with the hot cooked rice and adjust seasonings, if desired. Serves 6.

This casserole has all the makings of a meal, but the rich cheese sauce and scrambled eggs make it a perfect brunch dish.

This can be prepared entirely the day before, covered tightly and refrigerated to be baked just before serving.

WILD RICE BRUNCH CASSEROLE

3 cups cooked Wild Rice, about 2/3 cup uncooked
2 cups cubed, cooked ham
2 tbsp. butter
1 doz. eggs, lightly beaten
1/3 cup milk
3 tbsp. butter

For cheese sauce:
2 tbsp. oil
3 tbsp. flour
1 cup milk
2 cups grated Gouda cheese, about 1/4 lb.
1/4 tsp. powdered ginger
1/8 tsp. white pepper
Salt to taste
1 1/2 lb. fresh asparagus, cooked until just tender

Prepare rice and place in bottom of a lightly greased 9x11-inch, or similar shallow casserole. Saute the ham cubes in the butter just until ham begins to brown around edges. Place ham and pan juices in casserole on top of rice. Combine the eggs with milk; melt the 3 tbsp. butter in a skillet and scramble eggs just until they are soft. Do not cook until they begin to dry. Spoon eggs atop ham.

To make cheese sauce, heat the 2 tbsp. oil in a skillet and sprinkle the flour over the oil, stirring to blend in flour. Stir in the milk; cook and stir until sauce thickens slightly. Stir in the Gouda cheese, ginger, and white pepper. Add salt if desired.

Cook the asparagus and place this down the center of the casserole and spoon the cheese sauce over. Cover and refrigerate if casserole is to be baked later.

To bake, leave covered and bake at 325 degrees about 25 minutes, uncover and bake another 10 to 15 minutes, or until casserole is heated through. Serves 8 to 10.

Wild Rice can perk up everyday scrambled eggs making them something special for brunches.
SCRAMBLES WITH WILD RICE

1/4 cup each chopped celery and green pepper
2 tbsp. butter
8 eggs
1/2 cup half and half (light, or 2% cream)
1 cup cooked Wild Rice, about 1/4 cup uncooked
Salt and pepper to taste

Saute the celery and green pepper in the butter in a large skillet set over medium heat. Lightly beat the eggs with the half and half; stir in the wild rice. Pour into skillet and scramble until set, but still soft. Season with salt and pepper. Serves 4 to 6.

Whether you make this wild rice main dish to use up the hard-cooked eggs from Easter, or cook the eggs especially for this casserole, you'll like the results. With the crunchiness of the celery and the protein power of the eggs, this can be an entree for lunch or dinner.

EGG 'N WILD MAIN DISH

3 ribs celery, sliced
2 tbsp. butter
4 cups cooked Wild Rice, about 1 cup uncooked
3 hard-cooked eggs, chopped
1 (10½-oz.) can cream of celery soup
1/2 cup milk
1 tsp. salt
1/4 tsp. white pepper
1 cup buttered bread crumbs
2 hard-cooked eggs, sliced for garnish

Saute the celery in the butter about 3 minutes, just until celery begins to soften. Combine this with the wild rice and chopped hard-cooked eggs in a lightly buttered 2-qt. casserole. Blend the soup with the milk, salt and pepper and stir into the casserole with wild rice mixture. Sprinkle the crumbs on top and bake, uncovered, at 350 degrees for 20 to 30 minutes, or until casserole is heated through and bubbly. Garnish with the hard-cooked egg slices. Serves 6.

For a colorful main dish salad, stir up this ham and wild rice salad that's highlighted with chopped avocado and tomato. Served with corn chips, it makes a delightful luncheon or light supper.

WILD RICE SALAD
WITH HAM AND AVOCADO

3 cups cooked Wild Rice, about 2/3 cup uncooked
1 to 1 1/2 cups cooked, cubed ham
1 avocado, pitted and cubed
1 tbsp. lemon juice
1 large tomato, seeded and cubed
1/2 tsp. garlic salt
1/2 tsp. salt
1/4 cup Durkee's Dressing
3/4 cup mayonnaise
Lettuce leaves

Toss the wild rice with the ham, avocado which has been tossed with the lemon juice, and the tomato. With a rubber spatula, blend the garlic salt, salt, Durkee's dressing and mayonnaise. Gently fold this into first mixture. Chill several hours to blend flavors. Serve on lettuce leaves. Serves 4 to 6 as a main dish salad.

This egg salad-like creation, with wild rice, has a touch of brown sugar to add a bit of intrigue. Serve it, well-chilled, as a main dish salad.

SLIGHTLY SWEET WILD RICE SALAD

4 cups cooked Wild Rice, about 1 cup uncooked
1/2 cup brown sugar
3 tbsp. cooking oil
1 1/2 tsp. salt
1 small onion, chopped
1/2 cup mayonnaise
2 tsp. mustard

While the rice is still warm, toss it with the brown sugar, oil, salt, onion, mayonnaise and mustard. Cover and chill thoroughly and serve on lettuce leaves. Serves 4.

This delicate dessert, wild rice custard with a light lemon sauce, is as refreshing as it is nutritious. Count on it to supply part of your daily dairy products and protein needs.

WILD RICE CUSTARD WITH LEMON SAUCE

For custard:
2 cups milk
1 cup cooked Wild Rice, about 1/4 cup uncooked
1 tbsp. butter
1/4 cup sugar

1/4 tsp. nutmeg
1/4 tsp. salt
1/2 cup raisins or chopped nuts
1 tbsp. finely grated fresh lemon peel
2 eggs, lightly beaten
For sauce:
1/2 cup sugar
1 tbsp. cornstarch
1/4 tsp. nutmeg
Pinch salt
1 cup boiling water
1 tbsp. butter
2 tbsp. fresh lemon juice

To make custard, scald the milk and stir in rice and butter. Stir the sugar, nutmeg, salt and raisins or nuts and lemon juice into the eggs and slowly stir this into the hot milk, stirring constantly over low heat. Pour into a lightly buttered 1-qt. baking dish and set this in a pan of hot water—enough to come 1-inch up the sides of baking dish. Bake at 350 degrees about 40 minutes, or until custard is set; a knife inserted half-way between the edges of the custard and the center will come out clean.

For sauce, combine the sugar, cornstarch, nutmeg and salt in a small saucepan and gradually stir in the boiling water. Cook, stirring until thick and clear. Stir in the butter and lemon juice, stirring until butter melts.

While custard is still slightly warm, spoon into 4 dessert dishes and spoon lemon sauce on top. Serves 4.

Wild Rice with hard-cooked eggs, wheat germ, bean sprouts, green pepper and tomatoes makes a salad that's loaded with vitamins A, B, and C and protein. Try it on one of the first warm days of spring.

WILD RICE HEALTH SALAD

2 cups chopped hard-cooked eggs, about 8 medium
2 cups cooked Wild Rice, about 1/2 cup uncooked
1/3 cup wheat germ
1 cup bean sprouts
1 green pepper, chopped
2 green onions, sliced with some of the tops
1 tomato, chopped

For dressing:
1 cup yogurt
1 tsp. prepared mustard
1/4 tsp. salt
1/4 tsp. Maggi seasoning, optional

Lightly toss the hard-cooked eggs with the rice, wheat germ, bean sprouts, green pepper, onion and tomato. Combine the yogurt with the mustard, salt and Maggi seasoning, blending thoroughly. Lightly toss the dressing with the salad and serve on lettuce leaves. Serves 4 to 6.

The rich caramelly taste of this wild rice cookie comes from the brown sugar. But with the added nutrition of the wild rice and raisins, some of the calories of the sugar can be forgiven. Right?

WILD RICE COOKIES WITH RAISINS

2 eggs
1 1/2 cups (3 sticks) butter, softened
2 cups brown sugar
2 tbsp. water
1 tsp. vanilla
4 cups flour
1/2 tsp. salt
1 tsp. soda
1 cup cooked Wild Rice, about 1/4 cup uncooked
1/2 cup raisins

Cream the eggs, buttor, sugar, water and vanilla toget-her in a large mixing bowl. Add the flour, salt and soda, blending into the creamed mixture. Stir in wild rice and raisins.

Drop by rounded teaspoonfuls onto lightly greased baking sheets and bake at 350 degrees about 12 minutes, or until cookies are lightly browned. Makes about 6 dozen cookies.

When you have a bit of left over wild rice, combine it with cheese and onion to make these snappy hot appetizers.

CHEESY WILD RICE NIBBLERS

12 slices bread, crusts trimmed, each slice cut into
    3 (about 1x3-inch) strips
3 tbsp. butter, softened
1/2 cup cooked Wild Rice
1/2 cup finely chopped fresh mushrooms
1/4 cup finely chopped green pepper
1 small onion, finely chopped, not more than 1/3
    cup
1/2 cup grated Cheddar cheese
1/4 cup mayonnaise
1/4 to 1/2 tsp. Worcestershire sauce

Prepare the bread, making 36 oblong pieces. Spread with softened butter. Combine the cooked wild rice with the mushrooms, green pepper, onion, grated cheese and mayonnaise. Season with Worcestershire sauce, to taste. Broil the buttered bread until lightly toasted. Quickly spread with the cheese-wild rice mixture and continue to broil until heated through and bubbly. Makes 36 appetizers.

With a hint of bourbon and the crunchy texture added by the wild rice, this pound-cake is a sure winner. If you want to fancy it up, serve it with whipped cream, lightly sweetened and flavored with a splash of bourbon, piled in the center of the cake.

WILD RICE-BOURBON CAKE

4 cups sifted flour
1/2 tsp. salt
2 tsp. baking powder
1/2 cup bourbon
1/2 cup milk
2 cups (1 lb.) butter, softened
2 cups sugar
8 eggs, at room temperature
1/2 cup Wild Rice, cooked in unsalted water and only
    until the grains pop—do not overcook
1 tsp. vanilla extract

Sift the flour with the salt and baking powder. Set aside. Combine the bourbon and milk and set aside. Cream the butter and sugar together until light and fluffy. Add the eggs, one at a time, beating well after each. Alternately add the flour mixture with the bourbon-milk mixture, in 6 additions. Blend in the wild rice and vanilla, mixing thoroughly.

Generously butter and flour a 9- or 10-inch tube or Bundt pan. Pour batter into this and bake at 300 degrees 1¼ to 1½ hours, or until a straw or wooden pick inserted near the center comes out clean. Cool cake in pan set on rack about 10 minutes. Then turn cake out of pan onto rack.

To maintain maximum moistness in cake, place cake, not yet quite cooled, on a cake plate and cover. Cake is especially good served when not thoroughly cooled. but cool enough so that it will slice well.

Wild Rice
Recipes
for Summer

This quick wild rice saute, adapted from a recipe shared by Evelyn Belfour, Northport, Mich., makes a nice side dish to cook on the grill, along with steaks, chops or fish.

With the rice pre-cooked, the fixin's plenty quick. Simply saute the onion, mushrooms and green pepper in butter in a foil pie pan (or fashion your own container from a double layer of aluminum foil). Add the rice and seasonings and heat until rice is warmed through.

Of course, in other seasons, this works just as well indoors.

WILD RICE ON THE GRILL

4 to 6 cups cooked Wild Rice, about 1 to 1 1/2 cups
    uncooked
1 large onion, chopped
1/4 lb. fresh mushrooms, sliced
1 large green pepper, chopped, optional
1/2 cup (1 stick) butter
1/2 tsp. salt or seasoning salt
1/2 tsp. garlic salt
Pepper, as desired

Prepare the wild rice. Saute the onion, mushrooms and green pepper in the butter, seasoning as desired. Cook only until vegetables are tender, but still crisp. Add the rice; stir and when rice is heated through, serve. Serves 6 to 8, depending upon the amount of rice used.

Marilyn Nielsen, St. Paul, combined several recipes to come up with this company-sized casserole that's really nice with pork roasts or chops done on the grill.

NIELSEN'S APPLE-CHEESE
WILD RICE CASSEROLE

2 cups Wild Rice, cooked in chicken bouillon, according to basic or package directions
1 medium to large onion, chopped
5 ribs celery, sliced
1/4 cup water
2 (10½-oz.) cans cream of celery soup
1/2 cup grated Mozzarella cheese
1/2 cup grated Cheddar cheese
3 apples, cored and chopped, but not peeled

Prepare the wild rice. Simmer the onion and celery in the ¼ cup water about 5 minutes. Add this, with the water, to the rice. Stir the soup until smooth and stir this and the cheeses into the rice. Either on stove top or in a casserole in the oven, cook until heated through, 20 to 30 minutes. Add the apple pieces and continue to cook another 15 minutes. Serves 12 to 15.

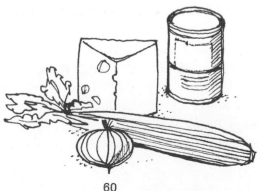

Mrs. Frank D. Alexander, Evansville, Ind. combines a touch of the Orient—soy sauce— with wild rice, a staple food of the Native Americans that live in Minnesota and Wisconsin.

SOY WILD RICE

4 cups cooked Wild Rice, about 1 cup uncooked
1/4 cup soy sauce
1/3 cup cooking oil
2 tsp. chopped onion
1/4 tsp. garlic salt
1/2 cup slivered almonds

Combine the cooked wild rice with the soy sauce, oil, onion, garlic salt and almonds, tossing to mix well. Pour into a lightly buttered 1½-qt. casserole and bake, uncovered 20 to 25 minutes at 350 degrees. Serves 4 to 6.

In Saffron Wild Rice, the world's most expensive grain, wild rice, is seasoned with the world's most expensive spice.

SAFFRON WILD RICE

3 tbsp. butter
1 onion, finely chopped
1 cup Wild Rice

1/2 tsp. crushed saffron threads, soaked in 1/4 cup
   lukewarm water for 15 minutes
3 1/2 cups water
1/2 tsp. salt

Melt the butter in a heavy 2-qt. saucepan and saute
the onion and the wild rice about 3 minutes, stirring
frequently. Add the saffron and the water in which it
has been soaked and the 3½ cups water and salt.
Bring to a boil. Cover and lower heat to maintain a
simmer. Cook about 40 minutes, or just until the
rice has popped. Fluff with a fork and cook, uncovered, to evaporate any excess liquid. Serves 6.

*Wild Rice spiced with just a touch of nutmeg is a nice
side dish to serve with fish or lamb.*

SPICED WILD RICE

4 cups hot cooked Wild Rice, about 1 cup uncooked
1 cup dairy sour cream
1/2 tsp. nutmeg
1/4 cup chopped water chestnuts, optional

Blend the hot cooked wild rice with the sour cream,
nutmeg and water chestnuts. Serve hot to 6.

This tomato-y creation is hearty enough to accompany pork chops or beef steaks done on the outdoor grill. With the rice and tomatoes in this main dish, all you need to add is a garden-fresh salad and a full-bodied red wine.

WILD RED RICE

1 medium onion, chopped
1 green pepper, chopped
6 to 8 tomatoes, cut-up
1/4 cup bacon drippings, or oil
1 tbsp. chili powder
1 tsp. sugar
1 tsp. salt
4 cups cooked Wild Rice, about 1 cup uncooked
1/2 cup grated Monterey Jack cheese

Saute the onion, green pepper and tomatoes in the bacon drippings, adding the chili powder, sugar and salt. Combine this with the rice in a lightly buttered 2½-qt. casserole. Sprinkle with cheese and bake, uncovered, at 350 degrees until cheese is melted and casserole heated through. Serves 6 to 8.

When fresh herbs are flourishing, either in your herb garden or at the supermarket, try this delicately seasoned rice. It will enhance the mild flavors of a veal roast or the freshest of fish.

HERBED WILD RICE

1/2 cup (1 stick) butter
2 tbsp. minced scallions
2 garlic cloves, minced
1 cup Wild Rice
2 bay leaves
1 tsp. fresh chopped thyme
1 tsp. fresh chopped basil
1 tsp. fresh chopped marjoram
3 cups chicken broth
Salt and pepper, as desired to taste

Melt the butter in a heavy 2-qt. saucepan. Saute the scallions, garlic and wild rice, stirring constantly until the scallions are limp, about 3 minutes. Add the bay leaves, thyme, basil, marjoram and chicken stock. Bring to a boil, reduce heat to maintain a simmer, cover and cook about an hour, or until the rice is tender. Remove bay leaves and discard. Fluff rice with a fork, and cook, uncovered, until any excess moisture is evaporated. Serves 4 to 6.

For warm weather menus when you want to serve something, but not much, hot, this filling and hearty casserole can be just the dish. It's nice to serve with a platter of cold sliced meats, or as a main dish with a tossed salad of garden vegetables and crusty French bread. And when it's the season, add watermelon wedges for dessert.

WILD RICE SPINACH BAKE

1 medium onion, finely chopped
1 (9- or 10-oz.) pkg. frozen chopped spinach,
   thawed and drained well
1 1/2 cups grated Cheddar cheese, about 1/3 lb.
1 1/2 cups cooked Wild Rice, about 1/3 cup
   uncooked
4 eggs, beaten until frothy
1 cup milk
1 tsp. salt

Combine the onion, spinach, cheese and wild rice, stirring to blend. Stir the eggs together with the milk and salt and stir this into the spinach-wild rice mixture. Pour into a lightly greased 1½-qt. casserole.

Set this in a pan with enough hot water to come up the sides of the casserole about an inch. Bake at 350 degrees 50 to 60 minutes or until the casserole is set in the center. Serves 6 as a main dish, more as a side dish.

Both indigenous to Minnesota, wild rice and walleye, complemented with a touch of dill, are sure to be popular in the Midwest.

If walleye is not available, substitute any fresh, mild-flavored fish fillets, like sole or ocean perch.

MINNESOTA WALLEYE AND WILD RICE WITH DILL

4 walleye, or other fish, fillets
2 cups light chicken bouillon
1 tbsp. lemon juice
1/4 cup (1/2 stick) butter
3 tbsp. chopped onion
3 cups cooked Wild Rice, about 2/3 cup uncooked
1/3 cup finely snipped fresh dill weed

Poach the fillets in the chicken broth and lemon juice, cooking just until the flesh will flake on the sides of fillets. With large slotted spatula, remove the fillets from the broth. Keep warm.

Melt the butter and saute the onion and wild rice briefly, just to soften onion and heat rice. Add ¼ cup of the fish-chicken broth and the fresh snipped dill weed, tossing lightly. Divide rice among 4 dinner plates and place fish fillets on rice. Serve with lemon wedges and a green vegetable, cooked tender-crisp. Serves 4.

When tomatoes and green peppers are garden-fresh, they'll be especially good in this pork chop casserole that's flavored with a touch of white wine.

PORK CHOP AND WILD RICE CASSEROLE
WITH WINE

4 loin pork chops
2 to 3 tbsp. oil
4 thick slices fresh tomatoes
4 thick slices Bermuda onions
4 circle slices green pepper
1 cup Wild Rice
Salt and pepper
1 cup dry white wine
3 cups water
Butter

Brown the pork chops in oil. Place in bottom of a greased shallow casserole, about 2½-qt. capacity. Place a slice of onion, a tomato slice and a green pepper ring on top of each pork chop, placing a tooth pick through the onion and tomato to hold in place. Sprinkle liberally with salt and pepper. Pour on wine. Cover with the wild rice. Add water to pan in which the chops were browned, cook, stirring from the bottom to loosen bits and pieces. Pour this juice over the rice, then dot with the butter. Cover and bake at 325 degrees about 3 hours. Serves 4. (This will hold well if dinner is delayed.)

This well-seasoned, elegant entree was shared by Jack Schweitzer, Minneapolis, Minnesota, who suggested that it be served with a chilled Chablis wine.

SHRIMP FRANCOISE ON WILD RICE

12 large raw shrimp
1 stick (1/4 lb.) butter, softened
2 cloves garlic, crushed
2 tsp. Worcestershire sauce
2 tsp. A-1 Sauce
1/2 tsp. Schilling all-purpose seasoning
12 (5-inch) pieces bacon
4 cups cooked Wild Rice, about 1 cup uncooked
Minced fresh parsley, for garnish

Split shelled shrimp half-way through down the back. Knead the butter with the garlic, Worcestershire sauce, A-1 Sauce and all-purpose seasoning. Shape the seasoned butter in a loaf and refrigerate to harden.

Partially cook the bacon by broiling about 2 minutes. Stuff each shrimp with a piece of the seasoned butter, then wrap securely with a piece of the partially cooked bacon. Broil bacon-wrapped shrimp 2 to 3 minutes.

Meanwhile, place cooked wild rice in a shallow, lightly greased casserole. Place shrimp atop the rice and bake in a 375-degree oven 10 minutes. Melt any remaining seasoned butter and drizzle over casserole. Garnish with minced fresh parsley. Serves 4.

Although this casserole is good anytime of year, it's especially nice in the summertime because it can be prepared ahead of time and baked when needed.

Double the recipe to feed a hungry crowd.

ROUND 'N WILD

6 cups cooked Wild Rice, about 1 1/2 cups uncooked
2 lbs. lean round steak, cubed
1/3 cup each vinegar and salad oil
1 tsp. Worcestershire sauce
3 garlic cloves, pressed
1 small onion, minced
3 tbsp. butter
1 (10-oz.) can cream of mushroom soup
1 env. dry onion recipe and soup mix
2 tbsp. sherry

Cook the wild rice, drain and set aside. Meanwhile, marinate the beef cubes in a mixture of the vinegar, oil, Worcestershire sauce, garlic and onion at least 4 hours at room temperature, turning meat several times. The meat can be marinated, covered, in the refrigerator overnight; the cooked rice also can be refrigerated overnight.

Drain the marinade from meat; reserve marinade for future use. Brown the steak cubes in the butter in a skillet set over medium-high heat.

To finish casserole, add the mushroom soup, dry onion soup mix and sherry to the browned meat, stirring to mix well. Add the rice and spoon into a 3-qt. lightly buttered casserole or shallow baking container. Cover and bake in a 325-degree oven about 30 minutes, or until heated through.

Or, the casserole can be completed, covered and re-frigerated to be baked later; bake, covered, at 350 degrees 30 to 40 minutes, or until heated thoroughly. Serves 6.

If you're a blue or Roquefort cheese-lover—or know of one, then this wild rice blue cheese side dish could be one you'd like. It's especially nice with a hearty steak or roast beef.

WILD RICE WITH BLUE CHEESE

3 cups cooked Wild Rice, about 2/3 cup uncooked
1/4 lb. fresh mushrooms, sliced
3 tbsp. butter
1/2 tsp. salt
2 to 3 tbsp. crumbled blue cheese

Prepare the wild rice. Saute the mushrooms in the butter about 3 minutes, or just until mushrooms are limp. Stir the wild rice, salt and blue cheese into the mushrooms and continue cooking until rice is heated thoroughly. Serves 4 to 6.

Ever wondered why hot, spicy foods are served in the warm climates? It's because the hot spices help keep you cool, some sources say.

Although the tomato sauce in this recipe is just hot and spicy enough for temperate palates, those of you who like it hot ... or hotter can add a few drops of Tabasco sauce.

Served with cooling cantaloupe wedges and soppipias with honey, Huevos Rancheros on the Wild make a brunch that's a bit unusual anywhere except in the Southwestern U.S. and Mexico.

HUEVOS RANCHEROS ON WILD RICE

3 cups hot cooked Wild Rice, about 2/3 cup
   uncooked
8 eggs
1/3 cup light cream
1/2 tsp. salt
1/4 cup chopped fresh parsley

For sauce:
1 cup ketchup
1/2 tsp. salt
1/2 tsp. garlic salt
1 tbsp. Worcestershire sauce
1/4 tsp. freshly ground black pepper
1 medium onion, finely chopped
2 tbsp. vinegar
1 tbsp. paprika
1/4 cup butter
Tabasco sauce, 1 or more drops to taste

Prepare wild rice according to basic or package directions.

Then make sauce by combining the ketchup with the salt, garlic salt, Worcestershire sauce, pepper, onion, vinegar, paprika and butter. Simmer, uncovered, about 20 minutes. Add Tabasco sauce to taste.

Beat the eggs lightly with the cream and salt. Scramble these in a small amount of melted butter, cooking just until eggs are set and still slightly soft.

To serve, spoon hot cooked wild rice onto four heated plates. Divide the scrambled eggs atop rice. Spoon sauce over the eggs and sprinkle with the chopped parsley. Serve immediately to 4.

A quick put-together, this tuna and wild rice salad can be the entree for a summer lunch or supper.

TUNA 'N WILD

3 cups cooked Wild Rice, about 2/3 cup uncooked
1 (6- to 7-oz.) can tuna, drained and flaked
1/2 cup sliced stuffed olives
1/4 cup chopped dill pickle
1/2 cup mayonnaise
3 tbsp. chili sauce
1 tsp. lemon juice

Toss the wild rice with the tuna, olives and pickles. Combine the mayonnaise with the chili sauce and lemon juice and blend well. Divide the rice-tuna salad into six portions atop lettuce leaves and spoon mayonnaise dressing on top. Serves 6.

Chippewa Rice combines wild rice, bacon and cooked egg strips in a brunch or supper dish that's sure to please. Serve it with sweet rolls and fresh fruit for brunch. And for supper, serve it with dinner rolls and a tossed salad, with fruit for dessert.

CHIPPEWA RICE

4 strips bacon
6 eggs, lightly beaten
1/4 tsp. pepper
1/2 tsp. salt
1/4 cup cream or milk
3 cups cooked Wild Rice, about 2/3 cup uncooked
2 tbsp. butter
2 tbsp. chopped fresh chives

Fry bacon in skillet. Remove bacon, drain and crumble. Stir the eggs with the pepper, salt and cream. Pour into skillet with bacon drippings, set over medium heat. Brown eggs lightly, without stirring. Turn as you would a pancake and brown other side. When firm, cut into strips and toss lightly with the cooked wild rice and crumbled bacon, heated thoroughly. Dot with butter and toss with the minced chives, tossing until butter melts. Serve hot to 4 or 6.

This souffle of wild rice, Gruyere and fresh parsley is light enough to be the highlight of a summer lunch or the side dish when the meat is beef on the grill.

WILD RICE SOUFFLE

1 1/4 cups grated Gruyere cheese, about 1/3 lb.
1 cup cooked Wild Rice, about 1/4 cup uncooked
1 cup fresh, chopped parsley
2 tbsp. butter
4 tbsp. flour
1 cup milk
3 large eggs, separated, or 4 medium eggs
1/2 tsp. salt
1/4 tsp. crushed tarragon
1 tbsp. sherry

Prepare the cheese, wild rice and parsley and set aside. Melt the butter in a skillet and stir in the flour. Slowly stir in the milk, cooking and stirring over low heat until sauce begins to thicken. Beat the eggs yolks until foamy and stir these, with the salt, tarragon, sherry and cheese into the sauce, cooking and stirring over low heat until cheese is melted and sauce thickened. Stir the wild rice and the parsley into this.

Beat the egg whites until stiff peaks form. Spoon about ½ cup of the beaten whites into the cheese sauce and fold in, blending well. Then, gently fold cheese sauce into the whites blending carefully but thoroughly.

Pour into an ungreased 1½-qt. souffle dish, or straight-sided casserole, and place this in a pan containing enough hot water to come up sides of casserole about an inch.

Bake at 350 degrees 45 to 50 minutes, or until souffle is risen and set. Serve immediately to 6.

Artichoke hearts, cherry tomatoes, peas and wild rice are dressed with a sherry-flavored oil and vinegar dressing to make this snappy salad. It's perfect for lunches or light summer suppers.

Tall glasses of iced tea and blueberry muffins are nice complements.

WILD RICE SALAD WITH ARTICHOKES

1 garlic clove, cut

3 cups cooked Wild Rice, about 2/3 cup uncooked

2 to 3 tbsp. minced scallions

1 cup cooked peas

10 cherry tomatoes, halved

1 (6-oz.) bottle marinated artichoke hearts, halved, reserve liquid

1/4 cup chopped fresh parsley

Salt and freshly ground black pepper, to taste

1/2 tsp. sugar

1 tbsp. sherry

Rub a large wooden salad bowl with the cut garlic, discard garlic. Toss the wild rice, scallions, peas, cherry tomato halves, artichoke heart halves and parsley with a generous sprinkling of salt and pepper. Stir the sugar and sherry into the reserved marinade from artichoke hearts, blending well. Drizzle this over salad, tossing to coat well. Serve 4 to 6 immediately.

Vine-ripened tomatoes filled with wild rice, with a hint of basil, are a cool and colorful go-together for cold sliced roast pork or beef. Add a garden-fresh green vegetable, a cool beverage and French bread for a summer dinner that can be prepared early in the day.

WILD RICE-STUFFED TOMATOES
WITH BASIL

4 large ripe tomatoes
1 1/2 cups cooked Wild Rice, about 1/2 cup
   uncooked
3 tbsp. chopped fresh basil
3 green onions, finely chopped with some of the
   green tops
2 tsp. olive oil
3/4 tsp. garlic salt, or to taste

Cut a 1-inch slice off the top of each tomato. Scoop out the inside pulp, being careful not to bruise the tomato shell. Chop the tomato pulp and drain excess liquid. Combine this with the wild rice, basil, onion, olive oil and gralic salt, tossing lightly. Fill scooped-out tomatoes with the rice mixture. Replace top tomato slices as "lids" if desired. Serve on bed of lettuce leaves. Serves 4.

VARIATION: Add about 1 cup flaked salmon to rice mixture and use as filling for 6 to 8 tomatoes.

Wild Rice, Green Goddess can be served either hot or cold. If serving hot, simply spoon the dressing at room temperature over the rice, being sure that the rice is very hot so that it stays warm.

To serve it as a salad, mound cooked, seasoned wild rice atop lettuce leaves and spoon green goddess sauce on top.

Either way, it's a different and tasty way to serve this unique grain.

WILD RICE, GREEN GODDESS

4 cups cooked Wild Rice, about 1 cup uncooked
For the green goddess sauce:
1 garlic clove, finely minced
1/2 cup chopped fresh parsley
1 green onion, chopped with some of the green tops
1 to 2 tbsp. anchovy paste, as desired
3 tbsp. tarragon vinegar
1 (12-oz.) carton dairy sour cream
Freshly ground black pepper, to taste

Prepare the rice. Blend the garlic, parsley, green onion, anchovy paste, vinegar and sour cream, adding pepper to taste. Serve the green goddess sauce, at room temperature over 6 individual servings of hot wild rice.

Or, for a salad, mound cold or room temperature wild rice on lettuce leaves and top with the green goddess sauce. Serves 6.

Dorothy Bendetti, Long Beach, California, must have a flourishing herb garden, for the wild rice recipe she shared calls for fresh dill, mint, chives and parsely— all of which add a refreshing, zingy taste to this Curried Wild Rice Salad.

CURRIED WILD RICE SALAD

3 cups cooked Wild Rice, about 2/3 cup uncooked
1/2 green pepper, chopped
1 cup chopped celery
4 green onions, finely chopped with some of the green tops
1 large bunch parsley, chopped
3 tbsp. snipped fresh chives
3 tbsp. snipped fresh mint
3 tbsp. snipped fresh dill
1 tsp. salt, about

For dressing:
1/2 cup olive oil
3 tbsp. fresh lemon juice
3 tbsp. red wine vinegar
3/4 tsp. Dijon-style mustard
1/2 tsp. curry powder

Combine the wild rice with the green pepper, celery, green onions, parsley, chives, mint, dill and salt, tossing gently to mix well. Combine the olive oil with the lemon juice, vinegar, mustard and curry powder for the dressing.

To serve, toss the dressing into the wild rice mixture and spoon onto lettuce leaves. Serve with cherry tomatoes or tomato quarters. Serves 6 to 8.

With pineapple, cottage cheese and wild rice, this lime-flavored gelatin salad is a summer salad luncheon special.

WILD RICE-LIME GELATIN SALAD

1 (8-oz.) can pineapple chunks cut in half; reserve juice
1 (3-oz.) pkg. lime-flavored gelatin
1 cup miniature marshmallows
1 cup cottage cheese
1 cup cooked Wild Rice, about 1/4 cup uncooked
1 cup whipped cream

Drain the pineapple chunks, adding enough water to reserved pineapple juice to make 1 cup liquid. Cut the pineapple chunks in half. Add the liquid to the gelatin and the miniature marshamallows, in a small saucepan. Cook over low heat until gelatin is dissolved and marshmallows melted.

Remove from heat and chill until almost set. Stir in the cottage cheese, wild rice and pineapple. Fold in the whipped cream. Refrigerate in an 8-inch square pan or in gelatin mold, until set. Serve on lettuce leaves garnished with a pineapple chunk and a lime wedge, if desired. Serves 6.

Wild Rice is one of the most nutritious and versatile of grains. Try it in this summer salad to enjoy an interesting, delicious combination of foods from both lake and ocean.

WILD RICE AND SEAFOOD SALAD

12 oz. cooked shrimp and/or crab
3 cups cooked Wild Rice, about 2/3 cup uncooked
Selected salad greens
2 green onions, chopped with some of the tops
2 tomatoes, cut into wedges
2 hard-cooked eggs, cut into wedges

For dressing:
1 cup mayonnaise
1/4 cup wine vinegar
1/2 tsp. dry mustard
2 tbsp. Dijon-style mustard

Toss the seafood with the wild rice. Chill well. Arrange salad greens on six individual salad plates or on serving platter. When ready to serve, toss the onions with the wild rice and seafood mixture and pile on lettuce leaves. Garnish with the tomato and hard-cooked egg wedges.

To make dressing, combine the mayonnaise with the vinegar, dry mustard and Dijon-style mustard. Stir until smooth and serve dressing atop the salad. Serves 6.

This filling salad, served with hard rolls and a white wine can make a summer lunch or dinner that needs only a bouquet of fresh fruits to make it complete... and memorable.

EGG 'N WILD RICE SUMMER SALAD

2 cups cooked Wild Rice, about 1/2 cup uncooked
4 hard-cooked eggs, coarsely chopped
1 rib celery, sliced thinly
1/2 green pepper, chopped
2 green onions, chopped with some of the green tops
1 tomato, peeled, seeded and chopped
1 cup mayonnaise, not salad dressing.
2 tsp. prepared mustard
1 tsp. salt
Lettuce leaves

Lightly toss the wild rice with the eggs, celery, green pepper, onion and tomato. Blend the mayonnaise with the mustard and salt and gently mix this with the rice-egg salad. Serve on lettuce leaves placed on 4 to 6 individual plates.

This very special wild rice summer salad has cashew nuts, green grapes and artichoke bottoms. Could it help but be very delicious?

GOURMET'S DELIGHT WILD RICE SALAD

3 cups cooked Wild Rice, about 2/3 cup uncooked
1 cup diced cooked chicken

1 1/2 cups green grapes, halved
1 cup cashew nuts
1 cup cooked and coarsely chopped artichoke bottoms, or substitute coarsely chopped water chestnuts
1 1/2 tsp. seasoned salt
1 cup mayonnaise, not salad dressing
Lettuce leaves

Have cooked wild rice either chilled or at room temperature. Combine this with the chicken, grapes, nuts and artichoke bottoms. Add the salt and mayonnaise and toss gently to blend thoroughly. Chill to blend flavors. Serve on lettuce leaves. Serves 6.

Cheesy Wild Rice Salad is the creation of Patricia Palmer Hanson, Rancho Santa Fe, California. With hard-cooked eggs, cheese and crunchy pecans, it makes a cool main dish for a hot day.

CHEESY WILD RICE SALAD

2 cups cooked Wild Rice, about 1/2 cup uncooked
4 hard-cooked eggs, chopped
1/4 cup pimiento-stuffed olives, sliced
1 cup diced longhorn (Cheddar) cheese
2/3 cup mayonnaise
1/4 cup pecans, chopped

Toss the wild rice with the hard-cooked eggs, olives, cheese and mayonnaise. Mix well. Can be covered and refrigerated for several hours at this point. Serve on lettuce leaves; sprinkle each salad with chopped pecans. Serves 4, generously.

The subtle flavors of mint and parsley enhance this crunchy wild rice summer salad. For fewer calories and a true Mid-Eastern taste, try the salad with plain yogurt.

MID-EASTERN WILD RICE SALAD

1 cup dairy sour cream or plain yogurt
1/2 envelope dry onion recipe and soup mix
1/2 cup chopped fresh mint
1/2 cup chopped fresh parsley
6 cups cooked Wild Rice, or about 1 1/2 cups
   uncooked
Freshly ground black pepper, as desired

Stir the sour cream or yogurt with the dry onion soup mix, mint, parsley, wild rice and pepper to taste. Refrigerate several hours to blend flavors. Serve as a salad on lettuce leaves. Accompany with fresh raw fruits and vegetables and crackers or bread—try pocket bread if it is available. Serves 6.

Cherry tomatoes scooped out and filled with a crunchy wild rice stuffing make tiny appetizer fare, just right for summer entertaining.

STUFFED CHERRY TOMATOES

24 cherry tomatoes
1 cup cooked Wild Rice, about 1/4 cup uncooked
1/4 cup finely chopped cashew nuts
1/2 tsp. Worcestershire sauce
1/3 to 1/2 cup mayonnaise
24 whole cashew nuts

Cut off the top ⅓ inch of the tomatoes and scoop out insides, leaving small tomato shells. Combine the wild rice with the chopped cashew nuts, Worcestershire sauce and mayonnaise. Use this to fill the tomato shells, placing a whole cashew nut on top of each. Cover and refrigerate until serving time. Makes 24 small appetizers.

With pineapple chunks, chutney, cashew nuts and green grape halves, this chicken and wild rice salad makes a summer meal all by itself. Simply serve on dark green lettuce leaves with whole grain muffins and an icy fruit juice drink.

POLYNESIAN SUMMER SALAD

2 cups cooked Wild Rice, about 1/2 cup uncooked
2 cups cooked, cut-up chicken or turkey
1 (8-oz.) can pineapple chunks, drained
1 cup green grapes, halved
1/2 cup coarsely chopped salted cashew nuts

For dressing:
1/2 cup mayonnaise, not salad dressing
2 tbsp. chopped chutney
1/2 tsp. salt
Lettuce leaves, for serving

Toss the cooked wild rice with the chicken, pineapple, green grapes and nuts. Stir the mayonnaise with the chutney and salt and carefully toss with it into the salad combination. Cover and chill several hours. Serve on lettuce leaves to 4 or 6.

If you keep hard-cooked eggs on hand during the busy summer season, you can stir up these Wild Rice Deviled Eggs in a jiffy. They'll rate raves from both family and guests.

WILD RICE DEVILED EGGS

8 hard-cooked eggs
1/2 cup cooked Wild Rice
1/4 cup chopped pimiento-stuffed olives
1/2 tsp. salt
Mayonnaise, about 1/4 to 1/3 cup
Sliced pimiento-stuffed olives, for garnish

Slice the hard-cooked eggs in half lengthwise. Squeeze each half gently to "pop" yolk out. Mash the yolks in a small bowl and stir in the cooked wild rice, olives, salt and mayonnaise, enough to moisten mixture. Stir until smooth and, using a tablespoon, fill egg white halves with the yolk-wild rice mixture. For a garnish, place a slice of pimiento-stuffed olive on top of each deviled egg.

Cover and refrigerate several hours before serving. Makes 16 deviled egg halves.

These crispy, do-ahead appetizer roll-ups are perfect for keeping on hand in the freezer. When you need a few snacks, pop these in the oven for a crispy treat, so nice with tall, cool summer drinks.

WILD RICE CHICKEN ROLL-UPS

1 cup cooked Wild Rice, about 1/4 cup uncooked
1 cup cooked chicken, finely minced
1/4 cup finely minced celery
1/3 cup mayonnaise
1/4 tsp. seasoned salt
1/8 tsp. white pepper
12 thin slices of bread, crusts trimmed
Softened butter
1/2 cup butter, melted

Combine the cooked wild rice with the chicken, celery, mayonnaise, salt and pepper. Spread the bread with butter, then with the chicken-wild rice mixture. Roll up llke a jelly roll. Wrap in plastic wrap. Chill or freeze. If frozen for storage longer than several days, wrap in aluminum foil.

To finish and serve, brush each roll liberally with melted butter. With a sharp knife, cut each roll into 4 bite-sized pieces. Place these, not cut-side-down, on baking sheet and bake at 400 degrees about 10 to 12 minutes, or until roll-ups are lightly browned. Serve immediately. Makes 48 appetizers.

For a breakfast bread that will stick to your ribs, even on busy summer days, try Blueberry Wild Rice Muffins.

BLUEBERRY-WILD RICE MUFFINS

1 cup cooked Wild Rice, about 1/4 cup uncooked
2 eggs, lightly beaten
5 tbsp. oil
1 cup milk
1 1/4 cups flour
1 tbsp. baking powder
1/2 tsp. salt
3 tbsp. sugar
1 cup blueberries

Stir the wild rice with the eggs, oil and milk. Sift the flour with the baking powder, salt and sugar. Stir the liquid ingredients into the dry, mixing thoroughly, but only until the ingredients are blended. Stir in the blueberries and spoon batter into 1½ doz. lightly greased muffin cups. Bake at 425 degrees 15 to 18 minutes, or until muffins are lightly browned.

VARIATIONS: Omit blueberries entirely or substitute chopped nuts, chopped rhubarb or well-drained pineapple for the blueberries.

When the blueberries are ripe, follow the Indian traditions and try blueberries with wild rice, for breakfast.

BLUEBERRY WILD RICE BREAKFAST

1 cup cooked Wild Rice, about 1/4 cup uncooked
1/2 cup blueberries
2 tsp. sugar
1/4 tsp. nutmeg
1/2 cup cream

Spoon the wild rice and blueberries into 2 cereal bowls and sprinkle with sugar and nutmeg. Pour cream over and serve. Serves 2.

When you want to make dessert count for more than something sweet, serve this topping over pudding, custard or ice cream. For an extra special breakfast treat, spoon it over cooked oatmeal or spoon it atop yogurt or enjoy it all by itself, like granola.

WILD RICE DESSERT TOPPING

1 cup cooked Wild Rice, about 1/4 cup uncooked
1/3 cup brown sugar, crumbled
1/2 cup raisins
1/2 cup chopped pecans

Combine the wild rice with brown sugar, raisins and pecans. Makes about 2 cups topping. This will keep, tightly covered and refrigerated, several days. Spoon over vanilla ice cream, pudding or custard.

For a nutritious summertime dessert, try this blue-berry-wild rice dessert combination.

WILD RICE-BLUEBERRY DESSERT

2 cups fresh or frozen blueberries
3/4 cup water
1/4 tsp. salt
3/4 cup sugar
2 tbsp. cornstarch
1/4 cup water
1 tbsp. lemon juice
3 to 4 cups cooked Wild Rice, 2/3 to 1 cup uncooked

Combine the blueberries, water and salt. Mix sugar and cornstarch and dissolve this in the ¼ cup water. Stir this into blueberries and cook, over medium heat, until thickened and clear. Stir in the lemon juice and then the cooked wild rice. Serve slightly warm or chilled, with whipped cream or vanilla yogurt as a topping. Serves 6.

Wild Rice adds a special nutty flavor to pancakes or waffles, makes 'em just right for breakfasts or late-night suppers.

WILD RICE PANCAKES OR WAFFLES

Fold ½ to 1 cup cooked wild rice into your favorite pancake or waffle batter. Finish and serve as usual.

*When you want something special—and homemade—
for breakfast or brunch, plan ahead and then, stir up
these Wild Rice Biegnets. They'll be perfect with
eggs, sausage and plenty of rich, brewed coffee.*

WILD RICE BEIGNETS

1 env. dry active yeast
1/2 cup lukewarm water
1 1/2 cups cooked Wild Rice, about 1/3 cup
  uncooked
3 eggs, well beaten
1 cup sifted flour
1/4 cup sugar
1/2 tsp. salt
1/4 tsp. nutmeg
Deep hot fat
Sifted confectioners' sugar

Soften yeast in warm water and stir in the rice, mixing well. Cover and let set several hours or overnight.
Add eggs, flour, sugar, salt and nutmeg. Beat well
and let stand in warm place 20 to 30 minutes. Drop
by tablespoon into deep fat, heated to 375 degrees
and fry until golden brown, turning to brown on both
sides. Remove and drain on absorbent paper. Roll in
confectioners' sugar and serve warm. Makes about 3
doz.

Wild Rice
Recipes
for Fall

If you've a busy social season and like to cook ahead and freeze to make entertaining easier, here's a terrific do-ahead recipe. It's from the recipe files of Mrs. Donald J. Nennd, Lake View, N.Y.

DO-AHEAD SHERRIED WILD RICE

1 cup Wild Rice
Boiling water
1/2 cup (1 stick) butter
1/2 cup slivered almonds
2 tbsp. finely chopped onion
1/2 lb. fresh mushrooms, sliced
1 tsp. salt
2 tbsp. sherry
3 cups chicken broth

Pour boiling water over the rice and let stand 1/2 hour. Repeat this and when cooled, drain rice well.

In a heavy frying pan, melt the butter and stir in the soaked and drained wild rice, almonds, onion, mushrooms and salt. Saute about 5 minutes, but don't let the onion and almonds brown. Stir in the sherry. Turn into a lightly buttered 2½-qt. casserole and pour chicken bouillon over.

At this point, the casserole can be covered and refrigerated or frozen.

When ready to serve, bring casserole to room temperature and then bake, covered, at 325 degrees an hour. Uncover and bake 15 minutes longer, or until rice is tender and liquid absorbed. Serves 6 to 8.

Norma Bachman, of St. Paul, Minnesota, uses this wild rice casserole, which freezes well when oven-ready, for wild duck or poultry dinners.

BACHMAN WILD RICE CASSEROLE

4 cups cooked Wild Rice, about 1 cup uncooked
1 small onion, chopped
1 (8-oz.) can mushroom stems and pieces
1/2 tsp. salt
1 scant tsp. poultry seasoning
1/4 tsp. pepper
2 tbsp. butter
1 (10½-oz.) can chicken broth or beef bouillon
Place the cooked rice in a greased 1½-qt. casserole. Saute the onion and mushrooms with salt, poultry seasoning and pepper in butter about 3 minutes. Add this with the chicken broth or beef bouillon to the rice in casserole, stirring well. Bake, covered, at 325 degrees for 30 minutes. Remove the cover, fluff with a fork and bake, uncovered, a few minutes longer, or until any excess moisture is absorbed. Serves 6 to 8.

(This recipe can be prepared up to the baking, then covered tightly and frozen. To bake, thaw and bake as directed, except uncover for the last half of baking time.)

This casserole of mushrooms, tuna and wild rice is nice for a crowd. It can be prepared in advance and refrigerated until you're ready to reheat and serve. The nutty flavors of the sauteed mushrooms and wild rice dominate, but the subtle flavor of the tuna enhances.

WILD RICE, TUNA AND MUSHROOMS EN CASSEROLE

6 cups cooked Wild Rice, about 1/2 lb.
1/2 lb. fresh mushrooms, sliced
1/2 cup butter
1 tsp. salt
2 (6½- to 7-oz.) cans tuna, drained and flaked

Prepare the wild rice. Saute the mushrooms in the butter until mushrooms are soft. Sprinkle with the salt. Combine with the rice and tuna and spoon into a lightly greased shallow casserole, at least 9x11-inches. Bake, covered at 350 degrees about 20 minutes, Uncover and bake another 10 minutes. Serves 10 to 12.

This wild rice side dish, crunchy with a lot of pecans, is a nice addition to almost any meal year 'round. But, it's especially good when the new crop of pecans is available in the Fall.

CRUNCHY PECAN WILD RICE

4 cups cooked Wild Rice, about 1 cup uncooked
1 onion, finely chopped
1 cup chopped pecans
4 tbsp. (1/2 stick) butter
1 tsp. seasoned salt
2 to 3 tbsp. fresh snipped parsley

Prepare the wild rice according to basic or package directions. Saute the onion and pecans in the butter in a small skillet, sprinkling the seasoned salt into this. Stir in the wild rice and cook until heated through. Adjust seasoning, if desired. Sprinkle with parsley. Serves 6 to 8.

This creamy casserole of wild rice and carrots will go well with game or poultry. And you can fix it early in the day and bake when needed.

CASSEROLE OF CARROTS AND WILD RICE

4 cups cooked Wild Rice, about 1 cup uncooked
4 slices bacon, cut-up
1 large onion, chopped
2 cups finely grated carrots
1 cup light cream
1 egg, lightly beaten
1 tsp. salt

Prepare the rice. Fry the bacon, remove and set aside. Saute the onion in the bacon fat until onion is lightly browned. Mix the wild rice with the bacon and carrots into the sauteed onion and bacon fat, stirring to mix well. Combine the cream with the egg and salt. Fold this into the rice mixture.

Turn this into a buttered 2-qt. casserole and bake, covered, at 350 degrees about 30 minutes. Remove cover, stir well and bake, uncovered another 10 minutes. Serves 6.

To do-ahead, prepare casserole and place in covered baking dish in the refrigerator. Increase baking time about 10 minutes, or until casserole is heated through.

This recipe for Orange Nut Wild Rice was shared by Sallie Flynn, Clinton, Maryland. It is a nice addition to the turkey and cranberry menu, so traditional at Thanksgiving.

ORANGE-NUT WILD RICE

1 small onion, minced
1 cup Wild Rice
1/4 cup (1/2 stick) butter
3/4 tsp. salt
2 cups water
Juice and grated rind of 1 large orange
1/2 cup chopped nuts

Saute the onion and wild rice in the butter in a heavy saucepan for 4 to 5 minutes. Sprinkle with the salt and add the water and orange juice. Bring to a boil. Reduce heat to maintain a simmer and cook, covered, over low heat about 45 minutes, or until rice has just popped. (For a crunchy, nut-like texture, do not overcook rice in this recipe.) Fluff rice with a fork and stir in the orange rind and nuts. Serve hot. Serves 6.

This stuffed flank steak is a meal that will please even those with the heartiest appetites. Sauced with a celery sauce, it needs only a vegetable and tossed salad to complete the meal.

By the way, the wild rice and sausage stuffing is good right by itself, so double the recipe and serve the rice as a side dish for one meal, then cover and refrigerate or freeze the other half to be used in the flank steak later.

WILD RICE-STUFFED FLANK STEAK

1/3 lb. bulk pork sausage, crumbled
1 medium onion, chopped
3 ribs celery, thinly sliced
1 tsp. crumbled leaf sage
2 tbsp. chopped fresh parsley
1/2 tsp. salt
1/4 tsp. freshly ground black pepper
2 tbsp. butter, optional
2 1/2 cups cooked Wild Rice, about 2/3 cup uncooked
Beef flank steak, about 1 1/2 lb.
2 tbsp. butter
1 (10½-oz.) can cream of celery soup
1 tsp. Kitchen Bouquet
1/2 soup can milk

Saute the sausage with the onion and celery, cooking until the sausage is lightly browned and the onions, limp. Stir in the sage, parsley, salt and pepper. If mixture is dry, stir in the optional butter. Add the rice, blending well.

Pound the steak slightly and spread filling down center of steak, leaving a little more than one-fourth of the steak exposed on each side of the stuffing. Bring edges of steak together and secure with string or wooden picks. In oven-proof container with cover, set over medium-high heat, melt butter. Brown steak on all sides. Remove from heat.

Combine the cream of celery soup with the Kitchen Bouquet and milk, stirring until smooth. Pour this over stuffed steak. Cover and bake at 350 degrees about 30 minutes. Transfer steak to heated platter, slice meat rolls. Serve sauce in separate container. Serves 4.

Wild rice goes Mexican in this colorful casserole. With its crispy topping of crushed corn chips, this is nice served with tortillas and guacamole for dipping. For a cooling dessert, serve vanilla pudding drizzled with a touch of honey.

WILD RICE MEXICALI

1 lb. ground beef
2 garlic cloves, minced
1 small onion, minced
1 tsp. salt
Dash or two Tabasco
1 cup dairy sour cream
3 cups cooked Wild Rice, about 2/3 cup uncooked
1 green pepper, chopped
2 medium tomatoes, cut into eighths, lengthwise
1 cup crushed corn chips

Saute the meat with the garlic and onion, breaking up into small pieces as it cooks. When meat loses its red color, drain excess fat and blend in the salt, Tabasco and sour cream. Stir in the wild rice, green pepper and tomatoes. Turn into a greased 2-qt. casserole and top with the crushed corn chips. Bake at 350 degrees about 30 minutes, or until casserole is heated through. Serves 6.

When you're cooking wild rice, make extra to use later in this Tuna-Wild Rice Loaf. It's a simple loaf that is nice served with fall squash (baked in the oven right along with the rice and tuna loaf) and a tossed salad.

WILD RICE AND TUNA LOAF

4 cups cooked Wild Rice, about 1 cup uncooked
1 (6 to 7-oz.) can tuna
2 ribs celery, sliced
1 medium onion, chopped
1/4 cup chopped parsley
3 eggs, beaten lightly
1 tsp. salt
1/8 tsp. pepper

Prepare rice. Drain oil from tuna into small skillet and saute the celery and onion in this about 3 minutes. Combine the tuna with the rice, sauteed vegetables, parsley, eggs, salt and pepper. Spoon into a lightly buttered 9x3x5-inch loaf pan and bake at 350 degrees about 45 minutes. Let set at room tempera ture about 10 minutes after baking. Slice to serve. Serves 4 to 6.

This meat loaf with wild rice and a cheese sauce is a filling entree for Fall family dinners. Add a green vegetable or coleslaw and baked apples to complete this simple, but delicious meal.

WILD RICE MEAT LOAF WITH
CHEESE SAUCE

For meat loaf:
1 lb. ground beef
3 eggs, beaten
2 cups cooked Wild Rice, about 1/2 cup uncooked
2 ribs celery, chopped
1 medium onion, chopped
3/4 cup chopped fresh mushrooms
1 tsp. salt
1/4 tsp. pepper

For cheese sauce:
2 tbsp. butter
2 tbsp. flour
1 cup milk
1 cup grated Cheddar cheese, about 1/4 lb.

Combine the ground beef with the eggs, wild rice, celery, onion, mushrooms, salt and pepper, mixing well. Pat into a 9x3x5-inch loaf pan and bake at 350 degrees for an hour.

To make cheese sauce, melt the butter over low heat and stir in the flour, blending well. Slowly stir in the milk, cooking and stirring constantly. Cook until smooth and thickened. Add cheese and stir until cheese melts.

When meat loaf is cooked, let cool in pan about 10 minutes. Drain excess juices from pan and turn meat loaf out onto serving platter. Slice and top with cheese sauce. Serves 6.

This simple, colorful recipe is a terrific accompaniment for turkey or chicken. Or, try it with roast pork

CRANBERRY WILD RICE

4 cups cooked Wild Rice, about 1 cup uncooked
1 (10-oz.) pkg. frozen cranberries with orange relish, thawed

Combine the cooked wild rice and the thawed cranberries in a buttered 2-qt. casserole. Cover and bake at 350 degrees 20 to 30 minutes, or until heated through. Serves 6.

Here are two ways to use those birds that often fill the freezers of hunting families in the fall. Duck Oriental with Wild Rice and Brandied Wild Rice 'n Duck Soup are companion recipes . . . you can cook the duck for both recipes at once.

When cooking the ducks, save yourself an hour and leave the pin feathers on; then peel the fat and skin from the cooked ducks and remove the meat for the recipes. Break the carcasses and use to make the duck broth for the soup.

If you have a microwave oven, microwave the ducks and then the broth to reduce both your time and the duck odors in the kitchen. Wash your hands in lemon juice to remove duck odor.

Two large ducks or three smaller ones will supply enough cooked duck meat for both recipes.

DUCK ORIENTAL WITH WILD RICE

3 green onions, sliced with some of the green tops
2 ribs celery, sliced diagonally
2 tsp. finely minced fresh ginger
1/2 cup slivered almonds
1/4 cup margarine
1 tsp. Beau Monde seasoning
1 tbsp. soy sauce
1 cup chicken broth (or use duck stock if available)
2 cups cooked Wild Rice, about 1/2 cup uncooked

2 cups diced cooked duck meat
1 (6-oz.) pkg. frozen Chinese pea pods, thawed, or
   use equivalent fresh
1/2 cup sliced water chestnuts
1 tbsp. cornstarch
2 tbsp. water
1 (11-oz.) can mandarin orange segments, drained

Saute the green onion, celery, ginger and almonds in
the margarine melted in a hot wok, or electric skillet,
about a minute. Add the Beau Monde seasoning, soy
sauce and chicken broth. Stir quickly and add the
cooked wild rice and duck, pea pods and water
chestnuts, stirring and cooking 3 to 4 minutes.

Meanwhile blend the cornstarch with 2 tbsp. water
until smooth and stir this into the mixture in wok,
stirring gently and briefly as liquids thicken slightly.
Add the orange segments and turn foods over once.
Serve immediately to 4. Pass additional soy sauce, if
desired. (The cooked wild rice also can be omitted
from the wok mixture and the duck-vegetable combo
served on beds of hot cooked wild rice.)

BRANDIED WILD RICE ' N DUCK SOUP

For stock:
2 duck carcasses, broken into pieces
1 large onion, sliced
2 ribs celery, sliced
2 carrots, chopped
1 tbsp. Maggi seasoning
1 1/2 qt. water   *continued next page*

For finishing soup:
1/2 cup (1 stick) butter
2 cups cooked Wild Rice, about 1/2 cup uncooked
1/4 cup blanched sliced almonds
2 medium onions, finely chopped
2 ribs celery, finely chopped
2 carrots, finely chopped
2 cups cooked diced duck
2 tsp. salt
1/4 tsp. white pepper
2 tsp. cornstarch
1 pint heavy cream
2 tbsp. brandy

To make stock, combine the duck carcasses with the onion, celery, carrots, Maggi seasoning and water in a soup kettle and bring to a boil. Reduce heat, cover and simmer about 1 1/2 hours. Strain. Cool broth, then refrigerate long enough to solidify fat. Remove all fat from broth.

To finish soup, melt the butter in a heavy soup kettle and briefly saute the wild rice, almonds, onions, celery and carrots, just until onions are transparent. Do not let vegetables brown. Add the soup stock, duck, salt and pepper and simmer, covered about an hour. Blend the cornstarch with a little of the cream, stirring until smooth. Stir this and the remaining cream into the soup and simmer until heated thoroughly. Stir in brandy and serve immediately. Makes about 4 qts. soup.

This Cream of Wild Rice Soup has a nutty-flavor that is especially nice in the fall.

WEBSTER'S WEST
CREAM OF WILD RICE SOUP

2 cups cooked Wild Rice, about 1/2 cup uncooked
1 large onion, diced
1/2 green pepper, diced
1 1/2 ribs celery, diced
2 large fresh mushrooms, diced, or 1 small can sliced
   mushrooms, drained
1/2 cup (1 stick) butter
1 cup flour
8 cups hot chicken broth
Salt and pepper, to taste
1 cup light cream, or half and half
1 to 2 tbsp. dry white wine, optional

Prepare the wild rice according to package or basic directions. Saute the onion, green pepper, celery and mushrooms in the butter about 3 minutes, or just until vegetables soften. Sprinkle in the flour, stirring and cooking until flour is mixed in, but do not let it begin to brown. Slowly add the chicken stock, stirring until all the flour-butter-vegetable mixture is blended well. Add the rice and season to taste with salt and pepper. Heat thoroughly, stir in the cream. Add the dry white wine, if desired. Heat gently, but do not boil. About 12 servings.

This wild rice stuffing, with extra flavor added by bacon, beef bouillon and mushrooms, goes well with turkey, chicken, pheasant or partridge. For those birds with heartier flavor, like ducks and geese, see the Sausage Stuffing suggestion below.

WILD RICE STUFFING

2/3 cup Wild Rice
3 cups water
4 tsp. instant beef bouillon granules
4 slices bacon
1 medium onion, chopped
1/2 lb. mushrooms, sliced
1 tsp. crushed leaf oregano
1/2 tsp. crushed leaf sage
3 ribs celery, chopped
2 cups bread crumbs
Salt and pepper, if needed

Run cold water through wild rice in a colander until water runs clear. Stir the rice into the water in a 3-qt. heavy saucepan and stir in the bouillon granules. Bring to a boil, stirring to dissolve bouillon. Reduce heat, cover and simmer until rice is tender, about 40 minutes.

Meanwhile, cut the bacon into 1-inch pieces and fry, adding the onion and mushrooms to saute with the bacon. Cook until the bacon pieces are crisp and the onions and mushrooms, softened slightly.

Add this to the cooked wild rice, along with the oregano, sage, celery and bread crumbs. Adjust seasonings with salt and pepper if needed. Makes enough stuffing for a 10 to 14 lb. turkey.

SAUSAGE STUFFING for ducks and geese which have more fat and robust flavor. Substitute one-half pound cooked crumbled and drained sausage for the bread crumbs. Adjust salt and pepper accordingly. This heartier stuffing goes well with ducks and geese and there are no bread crumbs or uncooked rice to absorb excess fat.

This casserole of Cheddar cheese and wild rice can be either a main dish or a side to go with roasts; it's especially good with roast beef or with steaks.

CHEDDAR 'N WILD RICE

4 cups cooked Wild Rice, about 1 cup uncooked
2 cups sliced fresh mushrooms, about 1/4 lb.
3 tbsp. butter
2 cups grated Cheddar cheese, about 1/4 lb.

Cook rice according to package directions, seasoning lightly with salt and pepper. Saute the mushrooms in the butter until the mushrooms soften slightly. Toss rice with the sauteed mushrooms and cheese and spoon into a buttered 2-qt. casserole. Cover and bake at 325 degrees about 20 minutes. Uncover and bake 10 minutes longer. Serves 4 as a main dish, up to 8 if used as a side dish with meat.

In the recipe below, a rich dough encases a filling of wild rice, spinach, cheese and walnuts. Served warm with the cheese sauce, it makes a showy meal for a fall buffet. Add a tossed salad and a basket of beautiful red apples for a simple, yet unique meal.

WILD RICE VEGETARIAN ROLL-UP

For pastry:
1 egg, lightly beaten
1 cup (2 sticks) butter, melted
3/4 cup lukewarm water
3 cups flour
1/4 tsp. salt
1 cup fine dry bread crumbs

For filling:
1 1/2 cups cooked Wild Rice, about 1/3 cup
   uncooked
1 small onion, finely chopped
1 (10-oz.) pkg. frozen chopped spinach, thawed and
   drained well
1/2 tsp. salt
1 tbsp. chopped parsley
1 cup shredded Swiss cheese, about 1/4 cup
1 cup small curd cottage cheese
1 cup finely chopped walnuts

For cheese sauce:
1/4 cup butter
1/4 cup flour
2 cups milk
1 cup shredded Swiss cheese, about 1/4 lb.

In a large bowl, combine the egg with 2 tbsp. of the melted butter and half of the water. Stir in half of the flour with all the salt, and then stir in remaining water and flour. Lightly flour hands and kneading surface; turn dough out and knead about 10 minutes. Shape into a ball, cover and let rest in a warm place about 10 minutes.

Meanwhile, mix the wild rice with the onion, spinach, salt, parsley, Swiss and cottage cheeses and walnuts.

Divide dough in half. Dust a large pastry cloth with additional flour. Place half the dough in center.

Flatten to a square and then roll out to an 18 inch square. Brush dough with butter and sprinkle lightly with bread crumbs.

Spoon half of the wild rice filling across one side of the dough, in a strip. Starting at the filled end, and using cloth to help roll, roll up dough tightly, jelly-roll fashion. Place on one side of a large, lightly greased baking sheet.

Repeat process with the remaining dough and filling; place on other side on baking sheet. Brush roll-ups with butter. Bake at 350 degrees for an hour, basting with melted butter every 15 minutes.

To make cheese sauce, melt butter and sprinkle in flour, stirring and cooking until flour is blended into butter. Slowly stir in milk, cooking and stirring until sauce thickens slightly. Add cheese and cook on low heat, stirring occasionally until cheese melts.

To serve roll-ups, slice into 3- to 4-inch pieces and serve with sauce spooned on top. Serves 12 to 14.

This recipe for pheasant—or you can use chicken or grouse—atop a creamy wild rice mixture bakes into a pretty casserole that will rate raves from dinner guests. Although it is baked uncovered, which makes the top a beautiful golden brown, the rice mixture is creamy enough to keep the pheasant moist. It was shared by Mrs. Don Taylor, Marshalltown, Iowa.

CREAMY WILD RICE WITH PHEASANT

6 cups cooked Wild Rice, about 1 1/2 cups
   uncooked
1 (10½-oz.) can cream of mushroom soup
1 (8-oz.) carton dairy sour cream
1 stick (1/4 lb.) butter
2 ribs celery, sliced
1 medium onion, chopped
1/4 lb. fresh mushrooms, sliced
1 tsp. salt
1/4 tsp. pepper
6 pheasant or chicken breast halves or thighs
1/4 cup (1/2 stick) butter
2 tbsp. lemon juice
1 tsp. Worcestershire sauce
3/4 cup evaporated milk
1 tsp. salt
1/4 tsp. pepper

Prepare the wild rice. Meanwhile, combine the soup with the sour cream, stirring to blend well. Melt the butter in a skillet and saute the celery, onion and mushrooms just until vegetables are slightly limp and onions, transparent. Stir in salt and pepper, sour cream-soup mixture and wild rice. Spoon rice into a lightly greased large, shallow baking casserole, about 3½-qt.

Wash the pheasant and pat dry with paper towels. Combine the ¼ cup melted butter with the lemon juice, Worcestershire sauce, evaporated milk, salt and pepper. Dip the pheasant pieces in this mixture and place these, in a single layer, over rice mixture, pressing pheasant pieces down into the rice, leaving just the top of meat visible. Bake, uncovered, at 350 degrees, 1¼ hours, or until meat is tender and lightly browned. Serves 6.

Wild rice with apples is just right to go with a pork roast on a crisp fall day.

APPLE-D WILD RICE

3/4 cup Wild Rice
2 1/2 cups strong chicken bouillon
2 red apples, unpared, but cubed
2 tbsp. butter
2 tbsp. warmed brandy, optional

Combine the wild rice with the bouillon, cover and bring to a boil. Reduce heat and simmer, covered, about an hour or until rice is tender. Add the un-peeled apple cubes and butter, toss lightly. Cover and continue to cook 15 minutes more. Spoon rice into a heated serving container; flame brandy and drizzle flaming brandy over rice, tossing lightly. Serve immediately to 4.

Apple-Roasted Ducks with Pecan-Wild Rice Dressing was created to please those who like a taste of something sweet with their duck. And the long-roasting at a low temperature assures tenderness, regardless of the age or type of bird.

The Pecan-Wild Rice Dressing also goes well with ducks roasted the conventional way, with only onion and bacon and served without a glaze. Shirley Banks, Paola, Kansas, shared the dressing recipe.

APPLE ROASTED DUCKS

1 small wild duck, or 1/2 large one, for each serving
Salt and pepper
Apples, 1/2 for each duck
Carrots, 1/2 for each duck
Onions, 1/2 for each duck
2 strips bacon for each duck
2 cups chicken bouillon
1 cup maple syrup
1 cup applesauce

Wash and clean ducks. Pat dry. Salt and pepper the cavities. Stuff 1/2 an apple, carrot and onion in each duck and place in a covered roasting pan. Lay bacon pieces over ducks and pour bouillon around. Cover and roast at 275 degrees about 5 hours for large duck, 4 for smaller ones.

Drain and discard liquid, remove stuffing and bacon and continue roasting, uncovered, about 20 minutes, or until skins begin to brown lightly. Combine the maple syrup with the applesauce. Increase oven temperature to 350 degrees and roast ducks, basting with the maple-applesauce mixture, 20 to 30 minutes, or until ducks are nicley glazed. Serve with the Pecan Wild Rice Dressing.

PECAN-WILD RICE DRESSING

3 cups cooked Wild Rice, about 2/3 cup uncooked
1 cup day-old bread crumbs, about 2 slices bread
1 medium onion, finely chopped
1 medium apple, not pared, but fincly chopped
1/4 cup (1/2 stick) butter
1/2 cup chopped pecans
1/2 tsp. poultry seasoning
1/2 to 1 cup chicken bouillon, more if needed

Combine the wild rice with the bread crumbs. Saute the onion and apple in the butter just until the onion is limp. Combine this, the pecans and poultry seasoning with the wild rice and bread crumbs, tossing to mix. Moisten with the chicken bouillon, using just enough so mixture will hold together.

Spoon dressing into a lightly buttered 1½-qt. casserole and bake, covered, at 350 degrees for 20 to 30 minutes. Uncover and bake another 10 minutes to brown top lightly, if desired. Serves 4 to 6.

(The dressing can be baked during the 30 minutes the ducks are being roasted at 350 degrees and glazed.)

This Wild Rice-Oyster Stuffing is nice with ducklings, from the supermarket, or wild ducks.

WILD RICE-OYSTER STUFFING

2 cups cooked Wild Rice, about 1/2 cup uncooked
1 small onion, chopped
2 strips fried bacon, crumbled
1/4 tsp. each sage and thyme
2 tbsp. finely minced fresh parsley
1 pint oysters, simmered in their liquid for 3 minutes
1/2 tsp. salt
1/4 tsp. pepper

Combine the wild rice with the onion, bacon, sage, thyme, parsley, oysters and their liquid, salt and pepper, tossing to blend well. Lightly fill cavities of 3 to 4 ducks, or a small turkey with this. Fasten opening and roast the fowl.

Or, place stuffing in a 1 1/2 qt. buttered casserole. Cover and bake 30-40 minutes at 350 degrees. Makes about 1 qt. stuffing, enough to serve 4.

Buffalo and Wild Rice is a stew that will bring out the "Wild West" in almost everyone. Serve it with plenty of steamed carrots and cabbage wedges with hot biscuits and honey.

BUFFALO AND WILD RICE STEW

3 lb. boneless buffalo meat, cut into 2-inch cubes
2 qt. beef bouillon
2 onions, peeled and quartered
1 tbsp. salt
1/2 tsp. freshly ground black pepper
1 1/2 cups Wild Rice

Place the buffalo, water and onions in a soup kettle. Bring to a boil, then reduce heat and simmer, covered, about 3 hours, or until buffalo is tender. Stir in the salt, pepper and wild rice. Cover and simmer about 30 minutes. Stir once, then simmer, uncovered about 20 minutes more, or until rice is cooked and most of the liquid absorbed. Serves 8.

VARIATION: Substitute venison for the buffalo.

Richly sauced and full flavored, this simple recipe does beautiful things for wild ducks. And it's so easy and delicious that you'll probably want to try it again and again.

BRANDIED DUCK BREASTS WITH WILD RICE

3 cups cooked Wild Rice, about 2/3 cup uncooked
1/4 lb. (1 stick) butter
1/3 cup brandy
1/3 cup sherry
1 tbsp. grape jelly
1 tbsp. Worcestershire sauce
4 duck breast halves, skinned and deboned
2 tsp. cornstarch
2 tbsp. water

In a heavy, covered skillet, melt butter and stir in brandy, sherry, grape jelly and Worcestershire sauce. Bring to a boil, stirring to dissolve jelly. Add duck breasts. Cover and reduce heat to low. Simmer duck 20 minutes, turning once.

Place hot, cooked wild rice on serving plates or platter and top with duck breasts. Cover and keep warm. Blend the cornstarch into the water, stirring until smooth. Add some of the hot brandy liquid to cornstarch mixture, then return this to sauce in skillet, stirring and cooking over low heat until sauce is thickened. Spoon sauce over duck breats on wild rice. Serve hot. Serves 4.

Wild Rice is a natural with game, so Janice Duvall, Jessup, Maryland, serves it topped with fried squirrel, with the pan juices poured over.

This same idea works well with fried rabbit or smothered venison steaks.

FRIED SQUIRREL WITH WILD RICE

2 squirrels, cut up
Flour
Salt and pepper
1/2 cup (1 stick) butter
4 cups cooked Wild Rice, about 1/2 cup uncooked
1/2 cup water
Freshly ground black pepper
Fresh parsley sprigs

Parboil the squirrel until tender in lightly salted water. Remove and drain. Season the flour with salt and pepper and dredge squirrel pieces In this. Fry squirrel in melted butter in heavy skillet, turning to brown on all sides.

Place cooked wild rice in a lightly buttered shallow casserole, about 8x12-inches. Arrange fried squirrel pieces on top. Add water to pan juices, cook on high heat, scraping up the bits and pieces from the bottom of the pan. Season to taste with freshly ground black pepper and pour this over the squirrel and rice. Warm in a moderate oven, if necessary, to keep rice and squirrel hot. Garnish with fresh parsley and serve Serves 4.

This combo of venison steaks and wild rice is season-ed only with pepper and the salt in a strong beef bouillon. This leaves the special flavors of both these natural foods unmasked so they can be enjoyed as nature intended them to be.

VENISON STEAKS WITH WILD RICE

4 venison steaks, round or sirloin
Red Wine
Freshly ground black pepper
Flour
Oil
1 cup Wild Rice
2 cups double strength beef bouillon

Marinate the venison steaks at room temperature in the wine at least 6 hours, turning frequently. Remove from wine and pat dry. Pound the steaks with liberal amounts of freshly ground black pepper. Dust the steaks with flour and brown quickly on both sides in a small amount of hot oil.

Stir wild rice with double-strength beef bouillon in a shallow, about 9x11-inch casserole. Place steaks over rice. Cover and bake at 300 degrees for an hour and a half. Uncover and continue baking until steaks are crispy on top and any excess liquid is evaporated. Serves 4.

Venison with wild rice is a dish that the Minnesota Indians enjoyed during the long cold winter. The recipe below is a modern-day venison and wild rice casserole, popular in the northern regions of Minnesota today. It's nice served with a cranberry salad and a green vegetable.

NORTHERN MINNESOTA VENISON AND WILD RICE CASSEROLE

4 cups cooked Wild Rice, about 1 cup uncooked
2 lbs. chopped venison
3 ribs celery, chopped
1 large onion, chopped
1 (8-oz.) can mushroom pieces, drained
3 tbsp. oil
1 can cream of mushroom soup
1/2 cup beef bouillon
1 tsp. garlic salt
1/2 tsp. sage

Layer the cooked wild rice in a buttered 3-qt. casserole. Saute the venison, celery, onion and mushrooms in the oil, browning the meat well. Blend the soup with the bouillon, garlic salt and sage. Stir the soup mixture into the sauteed venison and vegetables. Spoon this atop the wild rice. Bake, covered, 45 minutes at 350 degrees. Serves 6 to 8.

For a special meal, or a holiday meal when you don't want to cook a whole turkey, try Cornish Game Hens with this stuffing of wild rice, apricots and apples.

CORNISH GAME HENS WITH
FRUITED WILD RICE STUFFING

4 Cornish game hens
4 cups cooked Wild Rice, about 1 cup uncooked
2 apples, unpeeled, but cored and chopped
1 cup chopped dried apricots
1 cup chopped walnuts
1 tsp. each powdered ginger, nutmeg and salt
1/4 lb. (1 stick) butter, melted
Apricot preserves, optional

Thaw the hens, rinse well and pat dry. Combine the cooked wild rice with the apples, apricots, walnuts, ginger, nutmeg, salt and half of the butter. Toss lightly to mix well.

Stuff the hens with the stuffing and secure openings. Place any remaining stuffing in a small buttered covered casserole.

Place the stuffed hens in an open roasting pan and brush with some of the remaining butter. Place the casserole of extra stuffing in oven and bake both hens and stuffing at 350 degrees for 40 minutes, brushing hens with remaining melted butter from time to time.

Spoon the stuffing from casserole around the hens and spread the apricot preserves on hens. Continue baking another 15 minutes, or until hens are nicely glazed with the preserves and the stuffing, lightly browned. Serves 4.

This casserole combines the spicy flavors of sausage— and you can use as hot a sausage as you dare—with wild rice and squash quarters in a fall casserole just right for feeding a small crowd.

SQUASH AND SAUSAGE CASSEROLE WITH WILD RICE

1 cup Wild Rice
3 cups boiling water
1 lb. pork sausage, crumbled and cooked half of the time recommended on the label or just enough to render most of the fat; drain fat
1 tsp. salt, or to taste
2 large acorn squash, quartered lengthwise and seeded

Pour boiling water over rice and let stand about 10 minutes. Add the crumbled, half-cooked and drained sausage and salt, if needed. Pour this into a 9x13-inch baking pan or similar shallow casserole. Place squash quarters on top of sausage and rice; cover tightly and bake at 350 degrees 1½ to 1¾ hours. Serves 8.

For additional color, fill squash cavities with hot cooked brussel sprouts or peas just before serving.

This broccoli and wild rice casserole is a perfect do-ahead dish that goes well with almost any meat, fish or poultry entree. When asparagus is in season during the spring, try the same recipe with these delicate green spears.

LAYERED BROCCOLI WILD RICE CASSEROLE

4 cups cooked Wild Rice, about 1 cup uncooked
2 tbsp. butter
2 tbsp. finely chopped onion
2 tbsp. flour
1/2 tsp. salt
1 cup milk
1/2 cup dairy sour cream
6 broccoli stalks, cut in half, lengthwise, cutting through the flowerette
1 cup shredded Cheddar cheese, about 1/4 lb.
6 slices bacon, fried, drained and broken into small pieces (omit this for vegetarian main dish)

Melt the butter and saute the onion in the butter, stirring until onion begins to soften slightly. Sprinkle in the flour and salt, stirring and cooking over low heat until mixture is smooth. Slowly stir in the milk, cooking and stirring until the sauce thickens slightly. Fold the sour cream into this and blend into the cooked wild rice.
Steam the broccoli until just barely tender. Drain well. Layer half of the wild rice mixture in the bottom of a lightly buttered shallow oblong casserole, about 7x11-inches. Alternating the flowerettes towards the sides of the casserole, place the broccoli,

cut-side-down, on top of the rice. Spoon the remaining rice down the center of the broccoli. Sprinkle the cheese over the center of the rice and sprinkle bacon over both the cheese and the rice on top of the broccoli. Cover and refrigerate until ready to reheat.

To reheat, bake casserole, covered, about 20 minutes at 350 degrees; uncover and bake another 10 minutes or until cheese is bubbly and casserole is heated through. Serves 6 to 8.

Pork chops and apple slices give this main dish of wild rice and onion a fall flavor. Add crisp broccoli spears for a colorful, nutritious meal.

WILD RICE, PORK AND APPLE SKILLET

4 pork chops, about 1-inch thick
Oil for frying, as needed
1 cup Wild Rice
1 large onion, sliced into rings
2 1/2 cups chicken bouillon
2 large red cooking apples, cored and sliced

Brown the pork chops on both sides in an electric skillet set at 375 degrees, using as little oil as necessary. Remove chops and sprinkle rice in pan. Arrange chops and onion rings over the rice and pour chicken bouillon over this.

Bring to a boil, cover and lower heat to maintain a slow simmer, about 200 degrees, for an hour. Add unpeeled apple slices and simmer, covered, about 15 minutes more, until apples, rice and chops are tender. Serves 4.

The pretty gelatin salad of cranberries and wild rice can be a star at a salad luncheon. Or, it has all the flavors to go with a game dinner or a holiday meal.

WILD RICE CRANBERRY SALAD

1 (3-oz.) pkg. raspberry-flavored gelatin
1 cup boiling water
1 cup cranberry juice
1 (1-lb.) whole cranberry sauce, broken up with a fork
1 cup cooked Wild Rice, about 1/4 cup uncooked
Raspberry-flavored yogurt
Lettuce

Prepare gelatin, using the boiling water and cranberry juice, following package directions. Refrigerate in an 8-inch square pan about 30 minutes, or until gelatin is partially set, about the consistency of egg white. Stir in the cranberry sauce and cooked wild rice. Cover and refrigerate until firm. Cut into sections and serve, topped with raspberry-flavored yogurt, on lettuce leaves. Serves 9.

Gelatin can be prepared in a 1½-qt. gelatin mold with the yogurt passed separately. Or, blend the yogurt until smooth and use to frost salad squares or smooth-molded gelatin.

In this recipe, wild rice adds nutrition and its unique nut-like texture to a favorite old recipe.

WALDORF SALAD

2 cups cooked Wild Rice, about 1/2 cup uncooked
2 large Delicious apples
1 tbsp. lemon juice
2 tbsp. brown sugar
2 ribs celery, sliced
1/3 cup mayonnaise
1/2 cup dairy sour cream

Chill the cooked wild rice. Dice the unpared apples and toss with a mixture of the lemon juice and brown sugar. Stir in the celery and wild rice. Blend the mayonnaise with the dairy sour cream and toss this into the salad ingredients, mixing well. Chill thoroughly, but not longer than 6 to 8 hours. Serve on lettuce leaves to 6. Sprinkle with peanuts, if desired.

Wild Rice Cheese Balls can be prepared in advance, to be baked just before serving. Or, bake to be re-heated at serving time. This gives you, the cook, lots of flexibility.

These are nice served with spiced or mulled cider for casual fall social events.

WILD RICE CHEESE BALLS

1 cup cooked Wild Rice, about 1/4 cup uncooked
1 (5-oz.) jar Cheddar cheese spread
1 cup flour
1/2 tsp. baking powder
1/4 cup (1/2 stick) butter

Have all ingredients at room temperature. Blend together until a smooth paste-like consistency. Shape into 1-inch balls and refrigerate until chilled well. (These can be held at this point up to a week, or frozen for longer storage.) Bake at 350 degrees 10 minutes, or 12 to 15 minutes, if refrigerated. Bake about 20 minutes if frozen, or until cheese balls are puffed and lightly browned. Makes about 2 doz. Serve hot.

This beautiful brunch dish can be readied, but not put together, long before guests arrive. Then, at the last minute, assemble the casserole and pop into the oven.

BAKED EGGS IN CHEESEY WILD RICE

1/4 cup (1/2 stick) butter
1 cup sliced fresh mushrooms
1/2 cup chopped green pepper
3 tbsp. flour
1 tsp. salt
1/4 tsp. white pepper
2 cups half and half (2% or light cream)
1 cup shredded Swiss cheese
4 cups cooked Wild Rice, about 1 cup uncooked
8 eggs

Melt the butter in a skillet and saute the mushrooms and green pepper 3 to 4 minutes. Sprinkle in the flour, salt and pepper, stirring and cooking until blended well. Slowly stir in the cream, cooking and stirring constantly until mixture begins to thicken. Stir in the cheese and cook, stirring constantly until cheese is melted. Set off heat.

Stir 1/2 of the cheese sauce into the cooked rice. Spread this in a lightly buttered, shallow 7x11-inch, or similar casserole. Make 8 indentations in the rice. Spread a spoonful of the remaining cheese sauce in each indentation. Break an egg in each. Bake, uncovered, at 350 degrees 20 to 25 minutes or until eggs are cooked as desired.

When the crispiest apples ripen in early Fall, combine them with wild rice, maple or brown sugar and milk for this breakfast. It's so good you may not have any trouble getting up for breakfast again ... Unless, of course, you're a real sleepy head.

APPLE WILD RICE BREAKFAST

1 cup cooked Wild Rice, about 1/4 cup uncooked
1 unpared apple, cut into 1/2-inch cubes
1 tsp. butter
2 tbsp. brown or maple sugar
1/4 tsp. salt
1/4 tsp. cinnamon
1/2 cup cream, or as desired

Saute the apple in the butter in a small skillet set over low heat about 5 minutes. Sprinkle the brown sugar, salt and cinnamon over the apples and stir in the wild rice. Cook, stirring until rice is heated thoroughly. Divide between 2 cereal bowls and pour cream over. Serves 2.

The chewy, nut-like texture of wild rice makes it a perfect complement for this rich filling in this pie. With a crown of whipped cream, it's a fitting finale for a grand meal.

WILD RICE PIE

3 eggs, lightly beaten
1/2 cup brown sugar
3/4 cup light corn syrup
1/4 tsp. salt
1 1/2 cups cooked Wild Rice, about 1/3 cup uncooked
Pastry to line a 9-inch pie pan

Combine the eggs with the brown sugar, corn syrup and salt. Stir to blend well and stir in wild rice. Pour into the unbaked pie crust and bake at 350 degrees 40 to 50 minutes, or until center of pie puffs slightly. (It will settle after it cools.) Serve with whipped cream, if desired. Serves 6 to 8.

When you want to add pizzaz to your regular cooked breakfast cereal, try this suggestion.

WILD RICE BREAKFAST CEREAL

Stir cooked wild rice, about the same quantity as the cereal, into oatmeal or cream of wheat after you stir the cereal into the water. Finish cooking cereal according to package directions. Add raisins and brown sugar to taste. Serve hot with butter and cream if desired.

Like a rich bread pudding you may remember a favorite aunt or grandmother baking, this wild rice pudding has a rich full flavor, with just a hint of maple. It's a perfect dessert for a homespun supper on a chilly fall day.

MAPLE WILD RICE PUDDING

3 eggs, lightly beaten
1/2 cup brown sugar
1/4 tsp. salt
2 cups milk
1/2 tsp. maple flavoring
2 cups cooked Wild Rice, about 1/2 cup uncooked
3 slices stale whole wheat bread, cut into 1/2-inch cubes
3 tbsp. melted butter

Combine the eggs, brown sugar, salt, milk and maple flavoring. Toss the wild rice and bread in a 1½-qt. buttered casserole. Drizzle the melted butter over the rice and bread. Pour the egg-milk mixture on top. Set casserole in a pan of hot water, enough to come up sides of casserole about an inch, on a rack in the middle of an oven preheated to 350 degrees. Bake 40 to 50 minutes, or until custard is set. Serve warm, with lightly sweetened whipped cream or ice cream, if desired. Serves 6.

*The wild rice adds a special nutty flavor and texture
to this cake. It's nice served with the maple-flavored
whipped cream, below, or maple ice cream....or alone.*

MAPLE WILD RICE CAKE

1/2 cup (1 stick) butter
2 cups brown sugar
2 eggs
2 cups flour
1 tsp. soda
1/4 tsp. salt
1 cup buttermilk
1 tsp. maple flavoring
2 cups cooked Wild Rice, well drained, about 1/2 cup
   uncooked

Cream the butter with the sugar; add the eggs and
beat until smooth, light and fluffy. Mix the flour,
soda and salt together and add this, alternately with
the buttermilk to the creamed mixture. Blend in the
flavoring and the wild rice and pour into a 9x13-inch
well-greased and lightly floured cake pan. Bake at
350 degrees for about 25 minutes, or until cake
tests done. While still warm, cut into squares and
serve topped with the maple whipped cream, below.

MAPLE WHIPPED CREAM

1 cup heavy cream
1/4 tsp. maple flavoring
2 tbsp. sifted confectioners' sugar

Whip the cream until soft peaks form. Slowly beat
in the flavoring and the confectioners' sugar, beating
until cream is stiff, but still soft.

Wild Rice
Recipes
for Winter

A white sauce made in the old-fashioned way of thickening onion-flavored milk with bread crumbs is the unique part of this recipe, shared by Buell Hollister, Jr., Winnetka, Ill. It makes a hearty casserole that would go well with pork or beef roasts or with game. Hollister suggests that cranberry, currant or guava jelly is a nice accompaniment to this wild rice casserole.

HOLLISTER'S WILD RICE CASSEROLE

2 onions, quartered
8 whole cloves
3 cups milk
1/2 cup (1 stick) butter
1 tbsp. A-1 sauce
2 cups bread crumbs (use dry stuffing mix for additional flavor)
Salt and pepper, to taste, if needed
3 cups cooked Wild Rice, about 2/3 cup uncooked

Stud the onion quarters with the cloves and simmer over lowest heat setting with the milk and butter about an hour. Do not boil. Strain and add A-1 sauce and bread crumbs, adding bread crumbs gradually just to the consistency of a thick white sauce. Season to taste with salt and pepper. Stir in wild rice and spoon into a 2-qt. buttered casserole and bake uncovered at 350 degrees for 20 minutes, or until casserole is heated through. Serves 6.

If you have some cooked wild rice prepared in advance and set the spinach in the refrigerator to thaw during the day, you can put this filling main dish together in minutes. All you need to add to this for a simple dinner is a tossed salad and a fruit dessert, with French bread.

WILD RICE SPINACH MAIN DISH

4 cups cooked Wild Rice, about 1 cup uncooked
2 (9- or 10-oz.) pkgs. frozen chopped spinach, thawed
1 large onion, finely chopped
1 lb. ground beef
1 (16-oz.) jar process cheese spread
Salt and pepper to taste

Prepare the rice and thaw the spinach. Saute the onion and the ground beef, breaking up the ground beef, until beef loses its red color. Stir the cheese into this, stirring and cooking over low heat until cheese is softened and onion and meat blended in. Stir this with the wild rice and spinach into a 2½- to 3-qt. casserole. Bake, uncovered, at 350 degrees 45 to 60 minutes. Serves 6 to 8.

This wild rice casserole with ripe olives was shared by Sue Zelickson, Minneapolis, Minn. It's quick to fix and pop into the oven — and with a 2-hour, 325 degree baking time, it's a nice accompaniment for roasts.

WILD RICE CASSEROLE WITH OLIVES

1 medium onion, chopped
1/4 green pepper, chopped
1/2 lb. fresh mushrooms, sliced, or 1 (8-oz.) can mushrooms, drained
1/4 cup (1/2 stick) butter
1 (10½-oz.) can cream of mushroom soup
1 cup dry white wine
1/2 cup sliced ripe olives, or 2 (2¼-oz.) cans drained
1 tsp. celery salt
1 cup Wild Rice

Saute the onion, pepper and mushrooms in the butter. Stir the mushroom soup, wine, ripe olives, celery salt and wild rice into the sauteed vegetables, mixing well. Spoon into a lightly buttered 2-qt. casserole. Cover and bake at 325 degrees for 2 hours. Check during last half-hour of cooking, if casserole is too moist, uncover; if dry, stir in a bit more wine. Uncover during the last 10 minutes of baking to brown top lightly. Serves 4 to 6.

When Duck a l'Orange is on the menu, this wild rice, with just a touch of orange is the perfect accompaniment. Serve the Duck a l'Orange atop beds of Orange Wild Rice.

ORANGE WILD RICE

1 cup Wild Rice
4 cups chicken broth
3 tbsp. grated orange rind
2 tbsp. frozen orange juice concentrate, thawed

Cook the wild rice in the chicken broth, according to basic directions. Stir in the grated orange rind and thawed orange juice concentrate. Toss and serve hot to 6.

Variation: Cut oranges in half through the mid section, cutting a zig-zag design. Scoop out pulp and fill orange shells with orange wild rice. Heat just until rice is warmed. These are pretty served on individual plates or placed around beet or pork roasts, whole turkeys or roasted chicken or ducks. Allow 1 orange shell half per person.

Or, using a sharp knife, cut oranges to make baskets. Scoop out pulp and follow directions above.

On blustery cold winter nights when you'd like to serve a main dish with a cup of hot cream of tomato soup and a tossed salad, try this Cottage Cheese and Wild Rice Casserole.

COTTAGE CHEESE AND WILD RICE CASSEROLE

1 small onion, chopped
2 tbsp. butter
3 cups cooked Wild Rice, about 2/3 cup uncooked
1 (12-oz.) carton cottage cheese
1 (8-oz.) carton dairy sour cream
1/4 cup milk
Dash or two Tabasco sauce
1 tsp. salt
1/2 cup freshly grated Parmesan cheese

Saute the onion in the butter in a skillet and toss the cooked rice with this. In a mixing bowl, blend the cottage cheese with the sour cream, milk, Tabasco sauce and salt. Stir this into the rice and turn into lightly buttered 1½-qt. casserole. Sprinkle with the Parmesan cheese and bake at 350 degrees about 25 minutes. Serves 6.

You can warm most any winter evening by serving this casserole of wild rice, pork tenderloin and tomatoes. It's especially homespun when cooked and served in a large cast iron skillet or oven-to-table casserole.

TOMATO-Y WILD RICE CASSEROLE

6 pork chops or tenderloin slices
2 ribs celery, chopped
1 large onion, chopped
1 cup Wild Rice
1 1/2 tsp. salt.
1 tsp. sugar
1 (8-oz.) can mushroom stems and pieces and juice
1 (28-oz.) can tomatoes and juice

Brown the pork chops or tenderloins on both sides in small amount of oil. Layer the celery, onion and wild rice over the pork and drippings in oven-to-table covered casserole, at least 2½-qt. Sprinkle with the salt and sugar and add the mushrooms and tomatoes with juices. Stir all ingredients gently. Cover and bake at 300 degrees for 1½ to 2 hours, or until rice is tender and liquids absorbed. Serves 4 to 6.

For a meatless dinner, try wild rice patties, in a bun or served plain with a hot spaghetti sauce. This is, of course, an excellent way to stretch a bit of leftover wild rice.

WILD RICE PATTIES

2 cups cooked Wild Rice, about 1/2 cup uncooked
1/2 cup (about 1/8 lb.) grated sharp Cheddar cheese
2 eggs, lightly beaten
2/3 cup fine dry cracker crumbs
1 tsp. salt
Dash pepper

Combine the cooked wild rice with the cheese and eggs, stirring in 1/3 cup of the cracker crumbs, salt and pepper. Mix well and shape into 4 patties. Dip both sides of patties in the remaining 1/3 cup dry cracker crumbs and brown on both sides in small amount of oil in a skillet set over medium-high heat. Makes 4 patties.

When you bake winter squash, perk them up by filling the cavities with this wild rice combo.

WILD RICE-STUFFED SQUASH

2 acorn or buttercup squash, halved and seeded
2 cups cooked Wild Rice, about 1/2 cup uncooked
1/2 tsp. seasoned salt
2 tsp. grated orange rind
1 tbsp. brown sugar
1 cup chopped nuts
Apricot or orange juice, about 1/2 cup
2 tsp. brown sugar, optional

Fill the squash cavities with a mixture of the wild rice, seasoned salt, orange rind, brown sugar and chopped nuts. Bake, covered at 350 degrees for an hour, basting from time to time with the apricot or orange juice. When squash is tender, serve with ½ tsp. brown sugar sprinkled atop each wild rice-stuffed squash, if desired. Serves 4.

When you've got a bit of left-over chicken and ham, use it to make this specialty, Wild Rice Jambalaya.

WILD RICE JAMBALAYA

4 cups cooked Wild Rice, about 1 cup uncooked
1 large onion, chopped
6 slices bacon, cut-up
1 (8-oz.) can tomato sauce
1 cup diced cooked ham
1 cup diced cooked chicken
1 tsp. salt
1 tsp. crushed leaf oregano
Freshly ground black pepper, to taste

Saute the cooked wild rice, onion and bacon together, stirring often, about 5 minutes until the onion is soft and the bacon, partially fried. Stir in the tomato sauce, ham, chicken, salt, oregano and pepper. Cover and simmer together about 20 minutes to blend flavors well. Serves 4 to 6.

Before pilaf, there was pilau. That's an old Oriental word for a mixture of rice, blended with shrimp, chicken or other foods.

And while pilaf is probably more commonly used throughout much of the U.S., pilau is used in the coastal regions of the Southeastern U.S. to refer to such a rice dish.

This pilau is an interesting combination of wild rice, pistachio and pignon nuts, with a touch of mace.

WILD PILAU WITH NUTS

4 cups cooked Wild Rice, about 1 cup uncooked
1/4 cup pistachio nuts, with shells and inner skins
    removed
1/2 cup pignon nuts
1/4 cup butter
2 tsp. powdered mace

Prepapre rice and nuts. Melt butter in a heavy sauce-pan and toss both pistachio and pignon nuts in the hot butter and cook several minutes, stirring frequent-ly. Add the rice and mace and stir with a fork until heated through. Serves 6.

This recipe is a wild rice adaptation of the Creole Dirty Rice, popular in Louisiana. While chicken livers and gizzards are often used in the authentic Dirty Rice, with few seasonings other than cooking the wild rice in chicken broth, this recipe is made more interesting with parsley, onion, garlic, green pepper and celery.

WILD-DIRTY RICE

4 cups cooked Wild Rice, about 1 cup uncooked
1/2 cup (1 stick) butter
3 tbsp. flour
1 lb. chicken livers, halved
2 ribs celery, sliced
1/2 cup finely chopped fresh parsley
4 to 6 green onions, finely chopped
1/2 green pepper, chopped
3 garlic cloves, minced
1 1/2 tsp. salt
1/8 tsp. cayenne pepper
Freshly ground black pepper, to taste
1/4 cup chicken bouillon

In a large skillet or saucepan, melt the butter and sprinkle in the flour. Add the livers, celery, parsley, green onion, pepper and garlic. Stir and cook about 4 minutes, or until the livers lose their red color. Stir frequently, being careful not to tear livers. Add salt, cayenne and black pepper, if used, and bouillon; simmer, covered, on low heat 10 minutes. Fold hot cooked rice into the vegetables and liver. Adjust seasoning as desired. Heat thoroughly. Serves 6.

Combining a popular food of the South with the wild rice of the Midwest in this chicken gumbo creates a soup-bowl meal that's just right for weekend lunches or family meals on cold winter nights. Or, serve this to the Sunday afternoon football-watching crowd.

WILD RICE AND CHICKEN GUMBO

2 small onions, diced
2 tbsp. oil
1 (1-lb.) can tomatoes and juice
2 cups cooked okra, or 1 (9- or 10-oz.) pkg. frozen okra, thawed
2 cups diced cooked chicken
2 cups chicken broth
2 cups cooked Wild Rice, about 1/2 cup uncooked
1/2 tsp. paprika
Dash or two Tabasco
1 tsp. each sugar and salt
Freshly ground black pepper, to taste
Dash Cayenne pepper, if desired

Saute the onion in the oil and stir in the tomatoes and juice, okra, chicken, chicken broth, wild rice, paprika, Tabasco, sugar, salt, black pepper and cayenne, if you're brave. Heat thoroughly. Serves 4.

Pork chops with an orange wild rice stuffing is a specialty of amateur chef, Jack Schweitzer, of Minneapolis, Minn.

PORK CHOPS A LA SCHWEITZER
WITH WILD RICE

6 (2-inch thick) pork chops, with pocket cut on bone
  side
Salt and pepper
Milk and flour for coating chops
About 3 tbsp. fat or oil for sauteeing
1 cup cooked Wild Rice, cooked in chicken stock,
  according to basic or package directions
1/3 (6-oz.) can frozen orange juice concentrate,
  thawed
2 oranges, peeled, sliced and cut-up
1/4 cup honey
1/4 cup frozen orange juice concentrate, thawed

With a small sharp knife, cut a large pocket in the chops, from the bone side. Season chops with salt and pepper, dip in milk and then in flour. Brown the coated chops on both sides in hot fat or oil. Set chops aside while making rice stuffing.

Combine the cooked rice with the orange juice concentrate and cut-up orange slices. Fill each chop with about 3 tbsp. stuffing. Place stuffed chops in a heavy skillet. No liquid is needed in pan. Cover and roast in 350-degree oven 1 hour. During last 10 minutes of cooking, baste chops with a mixture of the 1/4 cup each honey and thawed, frozen orange juice concentrate. Serve chops with the remaining rice mixture, which has been heated thoroughly. Serves 6.

From Seattle, Washington, Edna Neupert sent this recipe for a pork chop and wild rice casserole, with onion and green pepper. If you brown the pork chops in a skillet that can go from stove top to oven and then, to the table, preparations and clean-up can be simple.

PORK CHOP AND WILD RICE CASSEROLE

1 cup Wild Rice
6 pork chops
1 medium onion, chopped
1 medium green pepper, chopped
1/2 tsp. salt
1/4 tsp. black pepper
2 beef bouillon cubes, dissolved in 2 cups hot water

Soak the wild rice in water several hours or pour boiling water over rice and let stand 30 minutes. Brown the pork chops on both sides in a small amount of oil in a large skillet. Place the pork chops in a greased 2½-qt. casserole or, if using the skillet for baking and serving, leave chops in skillet.

Drain the wild rice and scatter the rice over the chops. Add the onion and green pepper and sprinkle with the salt and pepper. Pour the bouillon over the top. Cover and bake at 350 degrees for an hour, or until rice is tender. Remove cover, fluff rice with a fork. If there is excess moisture, continue cooking until moisture evaporates. Serves 4 to 6.

Mrs. William. K. Meyer, Meridian, Mississippi, shared a recipe that had belonged to her mother, Mrs. William Lolley, Starkville, Mississippi, with the plea, "Please help me adapt this for serving to a large group." Here the recipe is increased to serve 20 to 30.

LOLLEY'S WILD RICE
AND SAUSAGE CASSEROLE

1 lb. Wild Rice, cooked according to package
  directions
1/2 lb. hot bulk sausage, crumbled, fried and drained
1/2 lb. fresh mushrooms, sliced
1 large onion, chopped
1 large green pepper, cut into 1-inch squares
6 ribs celery, sliced diagonally
2 (10½-oz.) cans cream of mushroom soup, undiluted
2 tsp. salt

Prepare the rice. Fry the sausage, remove meat from skillet and set aside. In fat remaining from sausage, saute the mushrooms, onion, green pepper and celery.

Combine the rice, sausage, sauteed vegetables, soup and salt, folding together thoroughly. Divide mixture into 2 (2-qt.) buttered casseroles. (This freezes well at this point.)

Bake, covered, at 350 degrees 30 to 45 minutes, or until heated through. If casserole has been frozen, thaw completely and then uncover during last half of baking time. Makes about 20 ¾ cup servings or about 30 ½ cup servings.

This casserole of wild rice, ground beef and vegetables is an entree suitable for family company meals. And it can be prepared in advance which makes it just right for busy winter days.

BURGER WILD RICE BAKE

1 large onion, chopped
3 ribs celery, sliced
1/4 lb. fresh mushrooms, sliced
1 green pepper, chopped
1 1/2 lb. lean ground beef, crumbled
1 1/2 cups Wild Rice
1 1/2 tsp. seasoned salt
1/2 tsp. freshly ground black pepper
1 cup white wine
3 cups chicken broth

Saute the onion, celery, mushrooms and green pepper with the beef, until beef loses its pink color. Combine this with the wild rice, salt, pepper, wine and broth in a lightly buttered 3-qt. casserole. Bake, covered, at 325 degrees for 2 hours. (This may be prepared in advance and frozen, to be cooked when needed.) Uncover last 15 minutes of baking if there is too much liquid. Serves 8 as a main dish or up to 12 as a side dish.

For busy wintry nights, when dinner should be warm and filling, this Beefy Bean Wild Rice Bake is a nice offering. Serve it with coleslaw, home-baked biscuits and a warm apple cobbler.

BEEFY BEAN WILD RICE BAKE

4 cups cooked Wild Rice, about 1 cup uncooked
1 lb. ground beef
1 large onion, chopped
6 slices bacon, cut-up
1 (1-lb.) can kidney beans, drained
1 (1-lb.) baked beans with juices
1/2 cup ketchup
1/2 cup brown sugar
1 tbsp. vinegar
1 tsp. salt
1 tsp. mustard
2 slices bacon

Prepare the wild rice. Brown the ground beef with the onion and bacon, breaking up the beef as it cooks. Drain any excess fat. Combine this meat-onion mixture with the wild rice and the kidney and baked beans, ketchup, brown sugar, vinegar, salt and mustard in a lightly greased 3-qt. baking dish. Lay the two slices bacon diagonally across the top of casserole. Bake uncovered, at 350 degrees about 40 minutes, or until casserole is bubbley and the top nicley browned. Serves 8.

This beef tenderloin recipe with an accompanying wild rice casserole makes a special meal for 12 people. Add a tossed salad with a variety of greens and a milk vinaigrette dressing, small dinner rolls and a cranberry sauce. For dessert, serve your favorite light dessert, with expresso coffee for a fabulous meal for entertaining.

BEEF TENDERLOIN WITH WILD RICE

1 (4- to 5-lb.) beef tenderloin
Kitchen Bouquet, or similar beef extract browning
   liquid
1 (10½-oz.) can beef bouillon

For wild rice:
6 cups cooked Wild Rice, about 1 1/2 cups
   uncooked
1/2 lb. fresh mushrooms, sliced
1 large onion, chopped
1/4 cup (1/2 stick) butter
1/4 cup flour
1/2 cup heavy cream
2 cups strong chicken bouillon
1 tsp. monosodium glutamate
1/8 tsp. each thyme, oregano and marjoram
1/4 tsp. pepper
1/2 cup chopped cashew nuts

Brush the beef tenderloin liberally with Kitchen Bouquet. Prepare the wild rice and saute the mushrooms and onion in the butter. Mix the flour into the sauteed mushrooms and onion. Stir the cream and chicken bouillon into this. Add monosodium glutamate, thyme, oregano, marjoram and pepper to this cream-bouillon mixture and cook, over medium heat, stirring constantly, until mixture thickens slightly. Blend this with the cooked wild rice in a 2½-qt. casserole.

About 30 to 40 minutes before serving time, preheat oven to 500 degrees. Place the beef tenderloin in an open roasting pan and pour the can of beef bouillon over the meat. Place this and the wild rice casserole in the oven and bake 20 to 25 minutes for rare, and up to 30 minutes for medium rare. Do not overcook the tenderloin. Baste meat with juices. Check to be sure rice casserole is heated through.

Spoon rice around the edge of a heated, large, oblong platter and place the tenderloin in the center. Sprinkle the cashew nuts over the rice and spoon any juices in the roasting pan over the tenderloin.

Slice and serve to 10 to 12.

Lots of celery, water chestnuts and a touch of soy give this skillet meal of wild rice and beef an Oriental taste. While the recipe is written for an electric skillet, this main dish can be baked, after the meat is browned, in a 300-degree oven for 1 1/2 to 2 hours. The celery and water chestnuts stay tender-crisp if added for the last 30 minutes of cooking, but if schedules make this impossible, put all ingredients in at once.

ORIENTAL BEEF AND WILD RICE SKILLET

1 1/2 lb. round steak cut into 1-inch cubes, or ground beef
Oil
1 cup Wild Rice
1 tsp. seasoned salt
1 (10½-oz.) can cream of celery soup
2 tbsp. soy sauce
1 medium onion, chopped
2 cups boiling water
2 cups sliced celery, about 4 ribs
1 (8-oz.) can water chestnuts, drained and sliced

Brown the meat in a small amount of oil in electric skillet. Add the rice, salt, celery soup, soy sauce, onion and boiling water. Stir to blend soup. Bring to a boil. Reduce heat to about 200 degrees, cover and simmer an hour. Add celery and water chestnuts, stirring well. Cover and continue cooking on low heat 20 to 30 minutes, or until rice and beef are tender, but celery is still tender-crisp. If liquid is excessive, uncover during this final stage of cooking. Serves 6 to 8.

This is the perfect recipe for the "second meal" after you've baked a turkey. Or, try it for those times when you need an easy-to-fix-ahead buffet dish for a small crowd.

TURKEY AND WILD RICE
BUFFET CASSEROLE

1 1/2 cups Wild Rice
1 heaping tsp. sage
2 tbsp. dry onion recipe and soup mix
1 (10½-oz.) can cream of celery soup
1 (10½-oz.) can cream of chicken soup
1 (10½-oz.) can cream of mushroom soup
2 soup cans milk
12 nice slices turkey

Place the rice in the bottom of a greased 9x13-inch baking pan, or similar container. Sprinkle the sage and dry onion recipe and soup mix over the rice. Heat the three soups with the milk, stirring until smooth and well-blended.

Reserve 1 cup of the soup-milk mixture. Lay the turkey slices on top of rice and pour the remaining soup-milk mixture over the turkey. Bake, covered, at 325 degrees 1½ hours. Uncover and bake 30 minutes more, or until rice is tender. Heat the reserved soup-milk mixture and use to spoon over individual servings of the casserole. Serves 6 to 8.

This traditional family favorite is even more delicious with wild rice and cashew nuts, both of which add crunchiness and texture.

GREEN PEPPERS WITH WILD RICE STUFFING

8 medium-sized green peppers
Salted water
For stuffing:
1/2 lb. lean ground beef
1 medium onion, finely chopped
1/2 tsp. dried basil
1/2 tsp. dried thyme
1/2 tsp. garlic salt
3 cups cooked Wild Rice, about 2/3 cup uncooked
1 cup chopped cashew nuts
1/3 cup each grated Parmesan and Cheddar cheese

Cut off and discard the top fourth of the green peppers. Remove the seeds and membranes. Place the **peppers upright in about ½ inch of salted water in** a heavy saucepan or kettle. Bring water to a boil, cover tightly, then reduce heat and cook 5 minutes, no longer. Remove the peppers and drain them cutside down on absorbent paper.

In a skillet, brown the ground beef and onion, breaking the meat into small pieces. Add the basil, thyme, garlic salt, wild rice, cashews and cheeses. Mix thoroughly.

Turn peppers right side up in a lightly buttered oven-proof container, placing peppers so that they are steady.

Fill pepper cavities with the wild rice stuffing. Bake, uncovered, at 350 degrees about 30 minutes, or until the stuffing is lightly browned on top. Serves 4, 2 peppers per serving.

This salmon and wild rice skillet supper can be readied in minutes, providing of course, that you have the cooked wild rice on hand.

WILD RICE SALMON SKILLET SUPPER

1 (2- to 3-oz.) can mushroom pieces, drained
3 ribs celery, sliced
3 tbsp. butter
1 (1-lb.) can salmon, drained and flaked
1 (10½-oz.) can cream of celery soup
1 soup can milk
1 tsp. soy sauce
4 cups cooked Wild Rice, about 1 cup uncooked
1 cup crushed chow mein noodles

In a large electric fry pan, saute the mushrooms and celery in the butter and stir in the salmon, sauteing several minutes longer. Blend the soup with the milk and soy sauce, stirring until smooth. Add this with the wild rice to the skillet mixture, stir to blend well and cook at 250 degrees about 20 minutes. Sprinkle each serving with crushed chow mein noodles. Serves 6.

This wintertime entree of oysters and wild rice makes a perfect buffet dish. Serve it with a green vegetable and cranberry sauce, maybe a tossed salad and a fruit dessert.

And for holiday meals, if you're not stuffing a turkey, this casserole makes a nice substitute with turkey rolls or roasts.

OYSTER-WILD RICE BAKE

1 small onion, chopped
3 ribs celery, sliced
1/2 cup (1 stick) butter or margarine
3 tbsp. flour
1/2 tsp. sage
1/4 tsp. each thyme and pepper
1/2 tsp. salt
1 cup milk
3 cups hot cooked Wild Rice, about 2/3 cup
    uncooked
1 pint small oysters, well drained
1/2 cup fine cracker crumbs
For mushroom sauce:
4 tbsp. butter
1/4 lb. fresh mushrooms, sliced
1/4 cup flour
1 cup each chicken bouillon and milk
1/8 tsp. each nutmeg, salt and white pepper

Saute the onion and celery in 1/4 cup of the butter. When vegetables are limp, sprinkle in the flour, sage, thyme, pepper and salt, blending well. Slowly stir in the milk and continue cooking until mixture thickens slightly. Stir in the rice and then put this into a well-buttered shallow, about 11x7-inch casserole dish.

Melt the remaining 1¼ cup butter and dip the oysters first in this and then into the cracker crumbs. Arrange these on top of the rice and sprinkle with any remaining cracker crumbs and melted butter.

Bake, uncovered, about 20 minutes at 400 degrees, or just until oysters begin to curl around the edges and brown lightly.

Meanwhile, make mushroom sauce. Melt the 4 tbsp. butter and saute the sliced mushrooms in this 2 to 3 minutes. Sprinkle in the flour, stirring to blend into the butter. Slowly stir in the chicken bouillon and milk, cooking and stirring constantly until mixture thickens slightly. Add the nutmeg, pepper and salt. Stir to blend. Serve in separate bowl to be spooned over the casserole. Serves 6 as a main dish, 8 to 10 if served as a side dish with meat or poultry.

Camouflaged in an entree with a Polynesian flair, this recipe's just right for using up any ham or turkey you might have left from the holidays.

POLYNESIAN WILD RICE MAIN DISH

3 cups cooked Wild Rice, about 2/3 cup uncooked
1 cup cooked cubed ham
1 cup cooked cubed turkey
1 (8-oz.) can pineapple chunks, reserve pineapple juice
1 green pepper, cut into 1-inch squares
1/2 cup sliced water chestnuts
1/4 cup butter
2 tbsp. soy sauce
1/4 tsp. garlic powder
1/4 tsp. pepper
1 tbsp. cornstarch

Combine the rice, ham, turkey, pineapple, green pepper and water chestnuts in a lightly buttered 2-qt. casserole. Melt the butter in a skillet and stir in the soy sauce, garlic powder and pepper. Blend the cornstarch with a small amount of the reserved pineapple juice and then stir the cornstarch mixture into the remaining pineapple juice. Stir this into the butter-soy mixture, cooking over low heat and stirring until mixture thickens slightly. Pour this over ingredients in casserole and toss to blend the sauce in well. Cover and bake at 350 degrees about 30 minutes. Serves 6.

This recipe was shared by Irene Deschampe, who uses the "precious wild rice" in stuffings for grouse or as a side dish with moose.

Mrs. Deschampe, who is of Chippewa ancestry, lives on the Grand Portage Indian Reservation in Northern Minnesota.

DRESSING WITH WILD RICE

2 cups cooked Wild Rice, about 1/2 cup uncooked
1 (1 1/2 lb.) loaf, day-old white bread, cut into 1-inch
  cubes
1 large onion, chopped
1 cup (2 sticks) butter
Chicken or beef bouillon, about 2 cups
1 tsp. each salt and ground sage
1/2 tsp. black pepper

Prepare the wild rice and bread cubes. Saute the onion in 1 stick of the butter and combine this with the wild rice, bread cubes and remaining butter, cut into 1/4-inch slices. Toss to mix and moisten with hot bouillon, using only as much as is needed to wet dressing ingredients well. Season with salt, sage and pepper.

Use as stuffing in poultry or game birds. Or, bake separately, in a covered, lightly buttered casserole, about 2½-qt., 30 to 40 minutes. Makes 8 to 10 cups stuffing.

Combine wild rice, which is grown near the small stream that is the beginning of the Mississippi River, with an adaptation of a popular Creole dish, Gumbo, from the area near the mouth of the Mississippi River ... and we have a wild rice gumbo that is nutritious, tasty and interesting. Served in a preheated soup bowl, with a well-made cornbread, it would make a winter evening meal worth remembering.

WILD RICE GUMBO

1/4 lb. bacon, cut into 1-inch pieces
1 (9- or 10-oz.) pkg. frozen cut okra, thawed
1 large onion, cut into rings
6 to 8 fresh tomatoes, coarsely chopped
1 tsp. each sugar and salt
Freshly ground black pepper, to taste
4 cups cooked Wild Rice, about 1 cup uncooked
Hot sauce, such as Tabasco

Fry the bacon, remove fried bacon pieces and drain. Saute the okra, onion and tomatoes in the bacon grease. Add sugar, salt and black pepper, cover and continue to cook vegetables over low heat about 10 minutes, until they are soft. Stir in the wild rice and **heat thoroughly. Add a few drops hot sauce, to taste. Serve in soup bowls, topped with the fried bacon pieces. Serves 4 to 6.**

VARIATION: To make the gumbo more of a soup, add tomato juice as desired. Heat thoroughly and season to taste. To make a cheesy gumbo, add about 1 cup grated sharp Cheddar cheese to the finished gumbo; stir to melt cheese slightly and serve.

For a filling, yet fancy soup that's a meal all by itself, try this Potato-Wild Rice Soup.

POTATO WILD RICE SOUP

1 tbsp. instant minced onion
1 cup water
1 (10¾-oz.) can cream of potato soup
1 cup half and half (light cream)
1 cup shredded Swiss cheese, about 1/4 lb.
1 cup cooked Wild Rice, about 1/4 cup uncooked
3 slices cooked, crumbled bacon

Put the instant onion and water in a 2- to 3-qt. heavy saucepan. Bring to a boil and boil, covered, about 3 minutes. Stir in the soup and blend until smooth.

Add the half and half, cheese and wild rice, and continue cooking, over low heat, until the cheese is melted and soup warmed. Divide soup in 4 heated soup cups or bowls and sprinkle the bacon on top. Serves 4.

Patty Laing, of Minneapolis, Minnesota, contributed the following recipe for a hearty winter soup.

HAMBURGER WILD RICE SOUP

1 lb. ground beef
2 cups cooked Wild Rice, about 1/2 cup uncooked
1 (10½-oz.) can cream of potato soup
1 (10½-oz.) can cream of asparagus soup (or cream of celery soup)
2 soup cans milk
1 cup shredded Cheddar cheese
Garlic salt, about 1 tsp., or to taste
Dried parsley flakes, about 1 tsp.

Brown the ground beef and drain. Prepare wild rice according to basic, or package directions. Combine the soups, milk and cheese and blend. Add wild rice and ground beef and simmer until the cheese has melted. Add garlic and parsley, adjusting seasonings to taste. Serves 4 to 6.

This is a favorite recipe for surviving Minnesota winters.

MINNESOTA WILD RICE SOUP

1 lb. ground beef
1/2 tsp. salt
1 tbsp. Italian seasoning
1 cup Wild Rice
1 cup water
3 drops Tabasco

2 tsp. instant beef bouillon granules
1/2 tsp. freshly ground black pepper
4 ribs celery, sliced
2 large onions, chopped
3 (10½-oz.) cans cream of mushroom soup
2 soup cans water

In a heavy, at least 4-qt. soup kettle, brown the beef with the salt and Italian seasoning, crumbling the meat as it cooks. Add the wild rice and water, Tabasco, bouillon granules, pepper, celery and onion and simmer about 30 minutes. Stir in the soup and soup cans water. Cover and simmer another 30 minutes. Adjust seasonings if desired. Serves 8 to 10.

Curried Wild Rice with raisins will complement a meal of pork or poultry. And, if you want to add a crunchy texture, stir in a few toasted slivered almonds.

CURRIED WILD RICE

3 tbsp. butter
1 medium onion, minced
1 green pepper, chopped
1/2 cup raisins
1 cup Wild Rice
1/2 tsp. curry powder
4 cups light chicken boulllon

Melt the butter in a 3-qt. saucepan. Add onion, green pepper and raisins and saute about 3 minutes, or until onions begin to soften. Stir in the rice, curry powder and bouillon. Bring to a boil. Cover and simmer over low heat about 45 minutes, or until rice has popped. Uncover, fluff rice with a fork, and continue cooking, uncovered, until any excess liquid has evaporated. Season with salt and pepper to taste. Serves 8.

Recipe Index

Quickie wild rice chicken bake, 31